A Journey of Faith: Moving from the Middle East to the West

Living in Two Different Cultures

Dr. Safwat Bishara

iUniverse, Inc.
Bloomington

A Journey of Faith: Moving from the Middle East to the West Living in Two Different Cultures

iUniverse books may be ordered through booksellers or by contacting:

iUniverse
1663 Liberty Drive
Bloomington, IN 47403
www.iuniverse.com
1-800-Authors (1-800-288-4677)

ISBN: 978-1-4620-2227-4 (sc)
ISBN: 978-1-4620-2228-1 (ebk)

Printed in the United States of America

iUniverse rev. date: 06/13/2011

TABLE OF CONTENTS

PART I EGYPT

PART II MOVING TO THE UNITED STATES

PART III IN THE UNITED STATES

PART IV BETWEEN TWO CULTURES: MIDDLE EASTERN AND WESTERN

DEDICATION

To my family: my wife and three daughters who made my life worth living.

EPIGRAPH

When you were born, every body was laughing—
but you were crying.

Live your life in a way that when you die, every body will be
crying—but you will be smiling.

Author unknown

PREFACE

"A Journey of Faith." But what is faith? It is to believe in something. Some believe in chance and coincidence—being at the right place at the right time. Others believe in their abilities: smartness, planning and control over their lives. Some believe in good deeds. Yet some believe in a higher power or authority that is sovereign. But even the last group divides along the lines of defining such a higher authority. Is it "Allah", Buddha, Intelligent Designer, or Jesus Christ the living God? Here too, some believe that He has already come but others believe He is yet to come.

To state here what the author believes in would be like putting the cart in front of the horse. The circumstances of my life led me in a certain direction. I do not think that I already had strong inclinations one way or the other that could have blindly influenced my final opinion.

This book tells about the occurrences that shaped my set of beliefs. I look back on my life and see some sort of a pattern. But at the time, it was not clear why things went one way or the other. With enough time and distance, however, a coherent picture emerged.

The following pages tell about how a mainstream family went through the changes, difficulties, and adjustments associated with moving from a Middle Eastern culture to a distinctly different Western society. At the time of moving, 1981, the parents were in their early forties, the three daughters ranged from 10 years old to seven months. Their vague memories about Egypt and eagerness to know about their heritage contributed to the author's motivation to write this book; the grandchildren may get a glimpse of their grandparents' homeland.

The names, times and lives of my family members are real. Several other people have touched our lives both domestically and overseas. To maintain their anonymity, however, their identities have been replaced by aliases.

On more than one occasion, a person appeared in our lives for a limited period of time, several months to a few years, only to move away and disappear. But such a short lapse of time would have quite an influence on our lives for many years afterwards, and sometimes led to a new direction either for one family member or for the whole family.

I should mention here that our overall experience has been positive. Though our lives went without flashy outcomes, the people who touched our lives contributed tremendously to make our journey a success.

There may be more than one way to explain the numerous situations where certain events happened in a certain way, or why a person temporarily appears in our lives and has an indelible impact. One might say it was just luck or coincidence. This might explain one or two instances, but, as the book reveals, it defies logic to use such reasoning to explain the many other occurrences when the unexpected took place at the expense of the normal and expected.

Recent events of the Middle East exacerbated the interest in the region's culture. Egypt lies at the heart of the region: geographically, historically, and intellectually. Egypt's regional footprints have been well noted and studied.

But culture can be elusive especially for an outsider. Studying or reading about a society is no substitute for personally living the culture. Born in Egypt, where the author lived for the best of 40 years, he grew quite familiar with the Egyptian society and its culture.

The author has personally lived the political, economic, and social developments that prevailed over the second half of the 20th century. Most information provided in this book are recollections of events the author has experienced. After moving to the United States, the author got feedback, about the Egyptian society, from extended family members as well as Egyptian newspapers available during visits to Cairo.

As an American citizen, the author has been living in the United States for over 30 years. Well-assimilated into the American culture, he lived the norms of social behavior. Familiarity with the two distinct cultures (the Middle Eastern, Egyptian and the Western, American) paved the way for a good understanding of each. NEWSWEEK and TIME magazines as well as Wall Street Journal were insightful resources for the political, economic, and social events.

ACKNOWLEDGMENT

The author thanks Dr. Jan Branthaver for his great help in editing the manuscript. His input in the areas of history and politics of the United States is invaluable. Before retiring, Dr. Branthaver was senior scientist at Western Research Institute (WRI), previously an institution of the United States Department of Energy.

PART I

EGYPT

CHAPTER 1

SEEDS OF DISCONTENT

In the early 1950s, Egypt had its National Research Center (NRC) completed. It was designed and equipped according to the most recent scientific technologies available at the time.

The NRC covered research fields that included chemistry, physics, geology, agriculture, engineering, and pharmacology—each field was represented by a number of specialized units, each unit staffed with at least one Ph. D. and a number of graduate students studying and preparing for their post-graduate degrees. At the time of moving to the United States in 1981, the NRC had over 2,000 research staff members not counting the administrative personnel.

At the helm of this new institution was the late Dr. A. Ryad Torky—a well-known Egyptian scientist who had completed his post-graduate work in a prestigious university in what was then West Germany.

Dr. Torky had published a considerable number (about two hundred) of research papers in peer-reviewed, international scientific journals in Europe and the United States. His world-wide reputation as an outstanding chemist helped the NRC to progress in many ways. The personal contacts he had established while in Germany, and Europe in general, facilitated the availability of scholarships offered by German, and other Western, institutions to young Egyptian scientists interested in pursuing post-graduate degrees.

The NRC grew appreciably during the 1950s. Over the years, full-time staff became increasingly available and new research areas were begun. The very early stages of the institution depended mainly on university professors who participated in overseeing the budding research activities.

Large numbers of college graduates were hired by the NRC, where they carried out research work under the supervision of the university professors. Some of these young graduates also applied for scholarships to study abroad for their M.S. and Ph. D. degrees. Egypt has mainly been open to the West, and many Egyptian scientists got their post-graduate degrees from European countries or the United States. Politics, however, would eventually interfere with this trend.

In 1956, however, and after some political developments, the late Egyptian president Gamal Abd-El Nasser nationalized the Authority of the Suez Canal—the 180-kilometer long water body that connects the Mediterranean Sea to the Red Sea. The significance of the Suez Canal for worldwide trade has always been recognized among politicians and world leaders. It is this fact in itself that led to the digging of this waterway late in the nineteenth century.

As Egypt nationalized the Suez-Canal Authority in Summer of 1956, the British-French administrative authority was abolished. The economic reality of losing profit from collecting fees imposed on tankers and ships crossing the Canal was compounded by the political and military considerations of the region. Britain and France planned a combined military invasion to regain control of the Suez Canal. But the late American president Eisenhower forcefully intervened, and the invasion forces eventually were withdrawn.

As a consequence of the tense political situation that prevailed at the time, many Egyptian students were redirected to countries within the Soviet Bloc to pursue their post-graduate studies, instead of Western countries.

To go back a few years, the peaceful military revolution of 1952 ended the monarchy in Egypt. Some military commanders were not happy with the king of Egypt (Farouk) and the political environment as a whole. On July 23, 1952 the country awake on the news that the military had usurped power. The king was allowed a safe exit to the exile in Italy where he lived till his natural death.

A couple of years later, Nasser got control of the Revolution Command Council (the controlling authority that held all power) and became the president of Egypt. Although the Revolution Command Council comprised of the 12 military officers who executed the 1952 revolution, Nasser was by far the most charismatic and powerful. A natural leader, he had the gift of captivating his audience. Nasser's ambitions did not stop at the Egyptian borders. His speeches increasingly addressed the other Arab countries, rallying them against imperialism.

In the late 1950s, and to strengthen the Egyptian economy Nasser decided to pursue the plans, designed years earlier, to build Aswan's High Dam. The Dam was expected to increase the cultivated land, and dramatically lower the price of electric power.

The Egyptian media, under the government's control, reported that the the United States decided to withdraw its financing of the Aswan High Dam project. Up to this point in time, the then Soviet Union had no political allies in the strategically-significant Middle East region. So, when Nasser, the emerging regional leader and president of an influential country like Egypt, expressed an interest in establishing economic relations and cooperation with the Soviet Union, his extended hand of friendship was immediately embraced.

The Soviets stepped in to build Aswan's High Dam, and Egypt entered an era of over 20 years of economic, political, and military cooperation with the Soviet Union. This period, though short in historical terms, had, and still has, far reaching socio-economic and political implications on the region and especially on Egypt.

A consequence of the evolving cooperation between Egypt and the Eastern Bloc was in the area of higher education. Late in 1956, the first group of Egyptian college graduates had their post-graduate admissions diverted from Western universities to institutions in the Soviet Union.

In the following years, others were sent to Hungary, Czechoslovakia, Romania, Bulgaria, and East Germany. By the 1960s the NRC in Cairo had seen a gathering of young educated professionals who returned back to Egypt, each after spending a number of years in practically every part of the developed world.

It was during those years when the author graduated from college, got a scholarship and joined the NRC early in 1960. A favored subject between us, as colleagues, was for those who were abroad to talk about the different aspects of life in the country where each had stayed and studied. It was not hard to grasp how members of the advanced countries dealt with each other, lived their lives and, most importantly, the underlying social fabric of these societies.

Although my colleagues' experiences covered different countries, some common observations became noticeably clear.

First, developed societies have a clear demarcation between work and leisure—when it is time for work it is hard work. By the same token, when it is time for leisure it is all fun and relaxation. Obviously in order to enjoy a vacation, financial resources must be available to allow the individual to participate. And for the citizen to have financial resources s/he must do his/her best at work. High productivity is reflected on the individual scale as well as the society as a whole. So, the cycle continues—hard work provides a good income which allows for good leisure time and a decent life. No wonder consumer consumption accounts for two thirds of the American economy.

But whenever the chain is broken, the whole process suffers. Imagine employees of a certain enterprise in a developed country who, right or wrong, consider themselves underpaid and begin slacking in their jobs. Productivity goes down, their compensation gets less, and the society as a whole is dragged down. Sounds like Economics 101.

The second characteristic of an advanced, civilized society is "trust." Although this may sound irrelevant, the effects of "trust," or the lack thereof, are far more reaching than one could ever imagine. With "trust" there is a lesser need to prove a claim—any type of claim. In a developing society where "trust" is lacking, if not absent, time and energy are spent to verify and prove a claim.

Instead of investing time and resources in production, developing countries waste resources to compensate for the "trust" that has been lost either between the individuals themselves or between the individuals and the ruling authorities. The author had seen and experienced how the lack of "trust" can drag a whole society down.

Consider a situation that is likely to take place in any society—developed or developing. A high-level government official or a corporate CEO was suspected of wrongdoing. In a democratic, developed country such an individual may be brought to justice. Any prior friends of the suspect are likely to distance themselves allowing justice to take place.

On the other hand, developing societies often look at a similar situation differently. Friends and relatives of the suspect interfere, trying their best to get him/her off the hook, even though they are probably sure that s/he is not innocent. When events like this become known and widespread, a society loses the "trust" and confidence both in the system as well as in other individuals. The ripple effect of distrust can not be overemphasized.

The third characteristic of a civilized society is the premise that every one is innocent until proven guilty. It is not hard to realize how this assumption of innocence is tied up to the second characteristic which is "trust." Because members of a society trust each other, the assumption of innocence would be inherent—and vice versa.

On occasions our discussions at the NRC touched on this subject and how a developed society looks at guilt and innocence. We used to joke saying: some communities consider every person to be innocent till proven guilty, but other societies treat its individuals as guilty until proven innocent. This, obviously, is somewhat an exaggeration but it still describes the general attitude in some developing countries. The government treats its citizens as untrustworthy, and the citizens do not have much trust in the government or the system as a whole.

Developed, democratic societies have built institutions to oversee the rule of law. The legislative, judicial, and executive branches of government are well established. In the United States the Constitution had "checks and balances" to guarantee against the usurpation of power by any of the three branches of government. It has rightly been said that: power corrupts and absolute power corrupts absolutely.

In addition to the three branches of government, a "fourth" one is the media. Inherent in its success, the media searches for anything that seems out of the ordinary—any suspected wrongdoing by an official, elected or appointed, or by a company executive. Whenever the underlying interest of a group—media executives and reporters, coincide with the overall benefit of a free society the whole system prospers.

Contrast this with a developing country where the media is mostly under the government's control and its role is significantly diminished. The degree of a government's control of the media is inversely proportional to the freedom of press in the society. A free press stands as a strong safeguard for the well being of the society. Courts can deal with libel suits if it becomes warranted.

In his book "Palestine—Peace Not Apartheid," N.Y., London, Toronto, Sidney: Simon and Schuster, 2006, pages 67 and 68, the 39th President Jimmy Carter notes:

> "When I travel in the Middle East, one persistent impression is the difference in public involvement in shaping national policy. It is almost fruitless to seek free expressions of opinion from private citizens in Arab countries with more authoritarian leadership, even among business leaders, journalists, and scholars in the universities."

Freedom of expression has been curtailed. The greatest danger is that it became so ingrained to be the norm.

The aforementioned is but a brief overview of the broad aspects of a Middle Eastern culture (represented by the Egyptian society) as compared with a Western culture (such as that of the United States of America). A more closer look at each of the two cultures seems a worthwhile undertaking. The author had the opportunity to be familiar with each of the two cultures. I had lived for 40 years in the Middle East (mostly in Egypt) before moving to the United States in March 1981, 30 years ago.

Chapters 18 through 25 present a modest attempt at revealing some characteristics of the two cultures.

CHAPTER 2

A HISTORICAL OVERVIEW

One way to understand the present is to look at the past. The culture of a nation is shaped, at least partly, by its history. For Egypt, this may not be easy as its history extends back to more than 6,000 years. Yet it is worthwhile trying.

ANCIENT EGYPT

The land of Egypt had seen one of the most ancient and sophisticated civilizations in the human history. A Travel Company, in an advertisement in the October 5th, 2009 issue of NEWSWEEK says: " . . . the scope of Egypt's vast magnificence and agriculture influenced the Greeks, Arabs, Romans and Christians."

Professor Bob Brier of Long Island University teaches a course about the history of ancient Egypt. The Great Courses Magazine, Chantilly, Virginia, in its 2010 edition, p. 33, announces the course and says:

> "Egypt was the most advanced of ancient civilizations . . . . The art of ancient Egypt is among the most beautiful of all ages . . . . The only one of the Wonders of the Ancient World still standing, the Great Pyramid of Cheops, was the tallest construction in the world until well into the 1800s . . . . Tens of thousands of men labored to raise the tomb—but they were not slaves; they were free farmers

> and artisans. The social organization of this project humbles most modern achievements."

Known as builders, the ancient Egyptians have built so many wonderful buildings that still defy time. The buildings, monumental statues and artifacts left by these people tell about a civilization characterized by ingenuity, dedication, and beauty. The design of the Great Pyramid is till today a matter of discussion. How it was built has always been, and continues to be, a subject of debate.

Even with laser beams and other state-of-the-art scientific tools available now, we are still unable to reach some of the inner chambers in the Pyramid. The thousands of limestone blocks, each weighing 5,000 pounds, used to build the Pyramid had to be cut from the mountain across the Nile river. To move each of these one-plus ton blocks for such a long distance from the mountain to the Nile then from the river to the building site on the Giza plateau, the ancient Egyptians were the first to invent the wheel.

Tree trunks were cut and the blocks were rolled over them. Then, the surfaces of each block were smoothed to perfection—to the point where the surfaces of adjacent blocks held together by vacuum; no cement was used. Not an easy job.

The magnificence and sophistication of the Great Pyramid have led some to say that "aliens" from out of space came to Earth and built the Pyramid. Assuming that is correct, how can we explain the existence of resources, statues, buildings and artifacts that extended over a period of more than 3,000 years of the ancient Egyptian history? Did these "aliens" stay for thousands of years on Earth? Why did they leave Earth after having invested such effort and time?

All the temples' walls depict ordinary human beings.

Not only did the ancient Egyptians excel in engineering, they were advanced in medicine and astronomy and developed the first form of government. On page 18 of the October 2002 issue of the National Geographic is shown a picture of some surgical blades that are "Sophisticated for their day, these 4,300-year-old bronze blades . . . . came from the tomb of a physician named Qar. A skull from another cemetery of the same period shows evidence of an operation, likely done with similar instruments."

The ancient Egyptians believed in the afterlife. On page 4 of the same issue of the National Geographic it says:

> "For 3,000 years kings and courtiers built lavish tombs at Saqqara which lies at the heart of vast burial ground. Showcases of wealth and power, the tombs expose the faith and vanity of those preparing for eternity."

> At Saqqara, " . . . . burials span the entire 3,000 years and 31 dynasties of the ancient Egyptian civilization . . . . Focusing on periods when the site was most heavily used by the rich and powerful, archaeologists are discovering evidence for the kind of cloak-and-dagger dramas that would make headlines today—conspiracies, assassinations, acts of revenge, scheming queens, ambitious politicians, and religious extremes . . . . And here [at Saqqara], the ancient Egyptians believed, was as close as mortal remains could get to the great beyond."

The reliefs on the walls of a mortuary chapel:

> "shows lines of servants presenting the tomb owner with baskets of produce, jars of beer, legs of beef, loaves of bread. Some of the reliefs still have traces of paint."

The ancient Egyptians believed that after death, a man's 'ka', or life force, "could return to this world through the figures in his tomb. He hoped relatives and priests would bring fresh offerings to sustain his ka."

In other words, the ancient Egyptians, 3,000 years B.C., believed in an afterlife. They believed in some sort of reincarnation as do now millions of people in the East (India) and increasingly in the West. They realized that life does not just end by death. Ancient Egyptians evidently believed in some sort of final judgment, as does

Christianity. This may explain why Egypt was quite receptive to Christianity in the first century A.D.

The long parade of ancient Egyptian kings ended in 332 B.C. when Alexander the Great conquered Egypt. "Foreign ways eroded the civilization that has risen to greatness along the Nile, but monuments in the desert endured, and daily life continued much as it had for millennium," reported the National Geographic.

In many aspects, this quote is accurate. Change has proved difficult in Egypt. Because of its geographic location the country was a point of attraction for the prevailing world powers. Invaders and occupiers were a constant. But the resistance for change, as negative as it is, helped keep the country together against all the dangers usually associated with foreign occupation.

CHRISTIANITY IN EGYPT

According to Tradition, around the year 62 A.D., St. Mark, the Apostle, arrived at the Mediterranean Sea port of Alexandria at the northern tip of Egypt. He preached Christianity and over the years the belief spread throughout the country. Churches and monasteries were built. And soon, Alexandria became the theological center of the Christian world.

The famous "Library of Alexandria" contained many of original documents—theological and otherwise. The value of such manuscripts can not be overemphasized. Long before the invention of printing, the original copy was the only and one available to humanity.

But, according to the teachings of Egyptian public schools, early in the third century A.D. the Library of Alexandria was burnt to the ground. Many believe it was arson. The crime against the human race went unpunished since no guilty party could be identified.

Was this the real story behind the destruction of the library? TIME magazine (September 20, 2010, p. 25) reported that early in the seventh century A.D. "... legend says, Caliph Omar burned some 200,000 objectionable books belonging to the library of Alexandria, warming the city's baths for six months."

Regardless of the culprit, the damage was done.

It should not be surprising that Egypt became the intellectual (and theological) center of the Mediterranean world. After all, the library belonged to heirs of the great ancient Egyptian civilization that extended for about 3,000 years, and built such wonderful monuments that still stand tall defying time and forces of nature.

It seems that the laws of nature are always at work. This may be true in the daily life of individuals as well as in the history of nations. A country gets to find out the right path to prosperity only to realize later that the same seeds of success carry with it the danger of decay. A particular civilization dominates over an era, then starts to decline, whereas another civilization is on the rise. And so on.

Maybe it is the divine will that no nation stays at the top forever. Human nature has its inherent flaws. This cyclical sequence allows the world forces to develop and interact. A civilization stays at the top for as long as it stays coherent internally. History proved this time and again.

The ancient Egyptian civilization started to decline around the year 300 B.C. Simultaneously, the Greeks were ascending the world scene. The conquests of Alexander the Great encouraged the spread of the Greek culture and language. Seventy two scholars meeting at Alexandria, Egypt, translated the Old Testament from the original Hebrew (Vorlage) to the Greek. The Septuagint Translation (285 to 270 B.C.) is the "Primary quoted text in the New Testament," stated Dr. Chuck Missler in his notes on "How We Got Our Bible," Koinonia House, 2005, p.8. Missler also reported on the "Coptic Versions" of the Septuagint Manuscripts that appeared in the third and fourth centuries.

For the New Testament, Missler, p.12, notes the following four historical omissions: 1—Nero's persecutions after 64 A.D., 2—Execution of James, 62 A.D., 3—Jewish Revolt against Romans, 66 A.D., and 4—Destruction of Jerusalem, 70 A.D. This may suggest that the writing of the New Testament has started before 60 A.D. and compiled within one lifetime.

The arrival of St. Mark to Alexandria around 62 A.D. is not mentioned in the New Testament which may also add to the hypothesis that writing of the New Testament has started before 60 A.D. Significant papyri were found at the Egyptian town of Oxyrynichus dated to 65 and 66 A.D. Dr. Carsten Thiede used a scanning laser microscope which can measure the height and depth of ink to differentiate between layers of the papyrus, as well as the angle of the stylus used by the scribe. Thiede compared the Oxyrynichus papyri with a "papyrus believed to be the oldest extant fragment of the New Testament [that] has been found in the Oxford Library .... It provides the first material evidence that the Gospel according to Matthew is an eyewitness account written by contemporaries of Christ," reported THE TIMES in its front page edition of December 24, 1994.

Comparing the Oxyrynichus papyri with the papyrus at Oxford Library led Thiede to conclude that "this is either an original of Matthew's Gospel, or an immediate copy, written while Matthew and the other disciples and other eyewitnesses were still alive," stated Missler, p.15.

A fifth century manuscript, the "codex Alexandrinus containing the entire New Testament was brought to England about 1630. Two centuries later, the "codex Sinaiticus" was discovered at St. Catherine's Monastery built on Mount Sinai, Egypt. "The manuscript, dated around 350 A.D., is one of the two oldest manuscripts of the Greek New Testament," said Missler, p.16.

So the evidence abounds concerning the early existence of Christianity in Egypt. Actually the intellectual and spiritual interests of the Egyptians in the afterlife extended back before Jesus Christ when the Septuagint translation of the Old Testament was completed in 270 B.C. The early New Testament Manuscripts: the Oxyrynichus papyri, the "codex Alexandrinus" and the "codex Sinaiticus" are all proof thereof.

Even the Gnostic heresies, aimed at twisting the truth, began in 55 A.D and the headquarters of the Gnostics later became Alexandria! The Gnostics mixed the Greek philosophy with the Revelation of God in His Son Jesus Christ. They advocated that all material is evil. Therefore, Jesus Christ was not God in the flesh but a phantom who left no prints in the sand. To achieve their goal the Gnostics mutilated the Scripture.

THE ADVENT OF ISLAM

For approximately six centuries, Christianity was the dominant religion in Egypt. In the middle of the seventh Century A.D. Egypt was conquered and occupied by the armies of the Muslim Arabs as they moved from Saudi Arabia westwards.

Islam spread across North Africa from Egypt to Libya, Algeria, Tunisia, Morocco and Mauritania. In Egypt, the invading Muslims gave the Christians the choice between two alternatives. 1—Pay a high tax (Gezya). 2—Convert to Islam. Those Christians who could afford paying the "Gezya" survived. But large numbers converted to Islam. These are facts taught in Egyptian high schools.

Today, the Egyptian constitution states that Shariah, Islamic law, is the basis of all legislation (Voice of Martyrs, August 2010). It is to be noted, however, that those six centuries during which Christianity prospered in Egypt are completely eliminated from the country's history.

During the author's middle and high school years, I learned nothing about this era. Schools do not touch on the subject in any way. By extension, Egyptian students learn but a little about the great ancient Egyptians—the forefathers of the early Christians. Such a civilization is in fact alien to the Islamic culture.

It may be possible to try to ignore the era of Christian dominance in Egypt, but it is much harder, if not impossible, to ignore the existence of the ancient Egyptian civilization with all of its colossal monuments. Millions from allover the world visit Egypt annually to see the wonders that such a civilization had left for the human race. Nowadays the tourism industry is the major source of Egypt's national income. One would wonder if it was not for the fortunes that tourism brings could this ancient civilization have been forgotten too?

EGYPT IN RECENT TIMES

The geographic location of Egypt has been a blessing as well as a curse. It occupies the north-east corner of Africa, with the Mediterranean

Sea to the north and the Red Sea to the east. The opening of the Suez Canal late in the nineteenth century added significantly to its strategic location. Trade between Europe and Asia found an enhanced route through the Suez Canal instead of routing all the way around South Africa to the Indian Ocean.

But even before the Suez Canal, Egypt attracted powerful nations that invaded the country during most of its history. In the late eighteenth century Napoleon invaded Egypt for a few years before the British navy forced him to leave. But in doing so, the French took with them a large number of skilled Egyptian workers.

The same policy was followed earlier by the Turks who occupied Egypt in the sixteenth century. The Turks, too, took many skilled Egyptian craftsmen.

If anything, this was a testimony to the efficiency and skill of the Egyptian worker. A skill that convinced the conqueror of his need for the conquered. The heirs of the "Great Builders" who built the Pyramids and Sphinx apparently did not loose their touch over thousands of years.

During the post World War II period (late 1940s) Egypt was the most powerful and prosperous Arab nation. The Egyptian pound traded for more than three dollars. The exploration of Mideastern oil, and the consequent rise in wealth and power of Libya, Saudi Arabia, and the Gulf States started in the early 1950s. Up to that point, Egypt was the leading political, social, and economic power in the region.

Egyptian doctors, engineers, college professors, judges, and craftsmen were provided and paid for by the Egyptian government to help neighboring countries. The Egyptian school teacher was ubiquitous all over the Sunni world at the time. Salaries and wages were the responsibility of the Egyptian authorities.

During the late 1950s and the 1960s, however, the Middle East saw many a political transformation with consequences that lasted for quite a long time—probably till today. Several political, economic and social events over a decade or two—a relatively short span of time in history, led, simultaneously, to the relative decline of Egypt and to the rise of oil-rich Arab countries.

In Egypt, the military usurped the power in a peaceful coup that ended an era in the recent history of the country. Prior to the "revolution" that took place on July 23, 1952, Egypt had a king with no official authority, and a prime minister who was elected and presided over the executive branch—similar to the system in the U.K. A congress with two chambers represented the legislative branch. Appointed judges constituted the judicial leg of governing. Members of the two-chamber congress were elected in a fair and timely manner. Political parties, as expected in a democracy, were active. The party that gathered the highest number of seats in congress had the privilege of selecting the prime minister who appointed his cabinet members (the American equivalent of Secretaries).

As in other democracies, the media played a critical role. Political parties owned or influenced the published material (no television yet existed).

On July 26, 1952 (three days after the "revolution") King Farouk was expelled from Egypt and left the country to live in Italy. The Revolution Command Council, initially presided by General Mohammad Naguib, took control. The political parties were abolished, and freedom of the press was critically curtailed. In 1954, Colonel Gamal Abd-El Nasser—a member of the governing Council took control and became the president of Egypt.

It has been reported that General Naguib did not actually participate in the planning or execution of the military coup. All members of the Revolution Command Council were rather of young age and lower military ranks. Having a General as the facade for the coup provided the needed legitimacy both domestically and abroad.

Later in 1954 and during a public speech at El-Manshia, Alexandria, an assassination attempt on Nasser's life failed. Shots were fired at him while delivering his speech. The perpetrator turned out to be a member of the Islamic Brotherhood. The event signaled the suppression of this extreme Islamic organization in Egypt for years to come. Nasser, the strong charismatic colonel who actually provided the planning and leadership for the 1952 military revolution, nearly exterminated the Islamic Brotherhood. He established the powerful and efficient "Mukhabarat," the equivalent of the CIA and FBI with its sphere of influence extending from the domestic to the foreign domains.

But at that time the effort was basically directed toward the internal security of the country. Many members of the Islamic organization were arrested and some managed to escape the country. Many fled to Saudi Arabia and other neighboring countries.

The Islamic Brotherhood started around the late 1920s as a small religious organization in Ismailia, Egypt, half way along the Suez Canal. Initially, the group sponsored some social activities, with no political ambitions. Even though Egypt at that time had a number of legitimate political parties, the Islamic Brotherhood remained just an organization and never attained the legitimate status of a political party. However, in Egypt, as is the case in almost all Middle Eastern countries, religion is the corner stone of the culture. It should not be surprising, then, to see such an Islamic organization grow in numbers and consequently in power.

Following the death of President Nasser, Anwar-El-Sadat became the president of Egypt. He was a great politician, if not so strong a leader as Nasser. Sadat had seen firsthand the futility of trying to pull the Arab nations together for a common cause. Nasser had dedicated his life and the resources of Egypt for such a policy. Time and again, this proved to be a dead-end road. (Part IV will further discuss this point.)

The short-lived merger with Syria ended in a bitter separation of the two countries. Defending Yemen by sending Egyptian troops there ended with defeat and cost Egypt billions of dollars—let alone the human casualties. The war in Yemen was the last straw, and Egypt's economy and infrastructure collapsed thereafter.

During Nasser's presidency, the late president Sadat was close to power as one of the twelve members of the Revolution Command Council presided over by Nasser. Sadat, a smart leader, apparently had settled on a different policy. An early sign, in retrospect, was his opening of a dialog between politicians, intellectuals, as well as those in the media about whether Egypt is an Arab state or a separate identity with roots extending back thousands of years in history?

One of the well-known and renowned intellectuals in Egypt, the late Dr. Lewis Awad, had compared what high school students in Egypt study about the Pharaohs with his/her counterpart in, yes, France. Dr. Awad was an Egyptian professor at Cairo University who authored a number of books.

In a two full page article published in Al-Ahram, the most widespread and respected newspaper in Egypt, founded in 1875, he reported that the French high school student ends up with several times more information about the ancient Egyptian civilization than the student in Egypt!

Some knowledgeable, responsible, and wise voices called for an "independent" Egypt. It was actually during this debate that Dr. Lewis Awad published the above-mentioned article pointing out that some European countries highly regarded ancient Egypt to the extent of its massive inclusion in their national educational curricula. Major American universities, such as the University of Chicago, has a whole department for ancient Egyptian history. But, as expected, the sheer number—not the logic, of those who advocated an Arab identity won the day.

This, however, did not deter Sadat. His initial plan of ending the long-standing Arab-Israeli conflict did not include any of the other Arab countries involved. Syria, Jordan, Lebanon and the Palestinians were taken by a complete surprise when Sadat went to visit Tel-Aviv. Signing a peace treaty with Israel led to two immediate results.

1. Egypt got all of its land—the Sinai Peninsula lost in the previous war, and 2. The 21-nation Arab League decided to move its headquarters from Cairo, where it has been since its inception in 1945, to the capital of an another North-African nation.

Anyway, the protest was short-lived, and the Arab League headquarters was moved back to Cairo where it still is. At the head of the Arab League, the Secretary General, is an Egyptian diplomat.

At a later stage during the negotiations at Camp David, where President Carter hosted both President Sadat and Prime Minister Began, the Palestinians were invited to share in the diplomatic effort underway. The period from 1978 to 1979 saw the signing of the first peace treaty between Israel and Egypt—the leading Arab nation.

The international community, especially in the West, was full of hope and the momentum for peace was never stronger. But as Abba Eban, foreign minister of Israel, said some people do not miss an opportunity to miss an opportunity. Interestingly, this applies to both sides.

The Palestinian leadership declined the invitation, and some angry voices blamed Egypt for even trying to include them in peace negotiations. Sadat's visit to Israel had taken the Arab world by surprise.

The "shock" had caused a lot of noise and uneasiness in the region. But the Egyptian authorities kept the country under control. This may have not been a difficult task after all. Since the establishment of Israel in 1948 Egypt had carried the brunt of the Arab-Israeli conflict and paid dearly both in man power and in money.

Culturally, during the decades from the 1920s through the 1950s the literature, arts and the media prospered in Egypt.

Intellectuals, authors, and singers contributed immensely to the cultural heritage. Nageib Mahfouz, born and grew up before the 1952 "revolution," won Nobel Prize in literature toward the end of the century. Dr. Taha Hussain was rightfully known in the Arab world as the "Dean of the Arabic Literature." Abbas Mahmoud El-Akkad, with no formal education, published books covering a wide range of topics, and his writings were deep and eloquent even to the educated reader. In poetry, Ahmed Shawky "Pasha" (a title offered to him by the royal palace due to his literary achievements) was widely known by all Arabic-speaking people as well as the media as the "Prince of the Poets." Um-Kalthoum was the most famous, respected and adored singer the region had seen over the second half of the 20th century. She sang many of Ahmed Shawky's poems combining eloquence in words with her powerful rich voice.

From the early 1950s till the late 1980s, that is for about 40 years, Um-Kalthoum had a live show the first Thursday of every month (Friday is the week-end in Egypt). Each month she would sing three songs, and each song lasted a minimum of an hour (sometimes as long as 90 minutes). Half-hour intermissions separated the songs. These approximately 500 shows were always booked to capacity well in advance. Quite a considerable number flew from neighboring countries, especially from Saudi Arabia and the Gulf States, solely to listen to Um-kalthoum. She was a country girl who started singing at the age of 10 but was nurtured by good people. She was the product of a healthy and proper environment.

After the failed assassination attempt on the leader of the young and popular revolution, the Muslim Brotherhood organization went underground but never completely died. After the passing away of Nasser in the early 1970s, President Sadat sought to derail the rapprochement between Egypt and the Soviet Union.

He unfurled the banner of "Education and belief." This implied the tacit approval of religious entities such as the Muslim Brotherhood. In just a decade they managed to infiltrate the Egyptian armed forces. Sadat was assassinated in the Fall of 1981 by a group of military personnel participating in the annual armed forces parade.

It has always been the case that during military parades, all weapons displayed and/or carried by soldiers have no live ammunition. The conspirators managed, however, to smuggle live ammunition that brought down the president of Egypt. It turned out that the Muslim Brotherhood was behind the assassination. Dozens of its members were captured and put to trial.

Saudi Arabia intervened with the Egyptian authorities and used its political influence to obtain the release of some of those on trial. Of those released a surgeon named Ayman El-Zawahry (not Zawahiri) was the most prominent. He left Egypt and went to Saudi Arabia, then to Afghanistan, where he became, and still is, the number two man of Al-Quaeda. El-Zawahry, in the author's opinion, is THE brains of Al-Quaeda—in addition to being the personal physician of Ben Laden.

El-Zawahry, M.D., came from one of the prominent, highly educated Egyptian families. His late father was the Dean of the College of Pharmacy at the University of Cairo. In the 1950s, his two uncles were full professors in the Medical School, Cairo University—one was a professor of dermatology and the other a professor of Obstetrics and Gynecology.

In Egypt, as it is in the United States, only the very top students are admitted to the Medical school, and a small number of the best graduating physicians are selected to pursue post-graduate work. In Egypt, El-Zawahry enjoyed social status, power and wealth.

How regrettable it is to see such human intelligence and potential dragged down into a failed and murderous life all in the name of Islam.

At the presidential stand overseeing the military parade of October 1981, Sadat had his vice-president Hosni Mubarak on his right. Miraculously, and for the good fortune of the country, Mubarak was slightly injured. Having seen and experienced firsthand the danger presented by (and as later proved) the Muslim extremists, Mubarak has always been on guard, exercising all his authority to keep the country safe from repeated attempts by extremists to overthrow the government and take control.

It might be appropriate here to emphasize a concept. Al-Quaeda is probably the most infamous among other similar organizations—all of them have a common denominator: jihad in the name of Islam. Some Muslims interpret that to simply mean a fight against oneself—against not obeying Allah. But "jihad in the name of Allah" has also meant to die defending Islam.

The early centuries of Islam had seen a number of wars where the Arabs of the Arabian Peninsula invaded several other countries. Early on, then, the "jihad in the name of Allah" became synonymous to Islam and its spread.

It is interesting to note that up to the 1950s Egypt, as a country, had seen a high level of tolerance. People of all the three main religions lived in great harmony together, each freely practicing his/her beliefs. Jews, especially in Cairo, owned some of the best and well-known department stores (Cicurel and Shamla) as well as other businesses. Christians enjoyed being represented in all three branches of government, up to the position of prime minister (Botros Ghali "Pasha," the grandfather of Dr. Botros Botros Ghali, the U.N. Secretary General in the 1990s). Makram Ubaid "Pasha," a Christian, was a distinguished, highly respected politician who was second only to Mustafa El-Nahhas "Pasha," the leader of the most powerful and populous political party (El-Wafd) in Egypt during the first half of the 20th century.

Banners with the crescent (symbol for Islam) and the cross together in unity was a familiar scene embraced by politicians as well as those in the media. Individual friendships at all social classes crossed the religion line without disapproval. The author's late father who was a physician had Muslims as most of his clientèle. The most prominent physicians in Egypt were Christian doctors. A patient never thought whether his doctor was a Muslim or a Christian so long as he was a good practitioner.

The 1950s, however, witnessed a gradual but definite change. Nasser had great hopes and good intention. But good intention is not always enough especially if coupled with some grave mistakes. He had humble beginnings. It is hard to tell whether this was behind his disdain for the rich people in Egypt and, by implication, the West in general that has symbolized wealth and prosperity? A specific incident might throw some light.

After Gamal Abd-El Nasser's graduation from high school he wanted to pursue a career as an officer and applied for the Military College (Academy). A large pool of applicants compete for a limited number of spots in the prestigious school. Having the right connections was a must; the more powerful your connection is, the higher would be your chances of acceptance. Nasser's stepfather (his biological father passed away when Nasser was a young boy) was working for a wealthy "Pasha" who agreed to accompany Nasser to talk to an official who would directly or indirectly be involved in the interviewing and selection process.

The "Pasha" rode in the back seat of his car and when Gamal tried to climb and sit beside him, he was ordered to sit in the front seat next to the driver. The future president never forgot this incident.

A single occurrence like that might not adequately explain the political, economic and social policies that Nasser followed during his presidency of sixteen years from 1954 till 1970. Some events on the international stage might also have interfered.

Up to the 1950s, Egypt was basically allied with the U.K. Even though the two countries signed a treaty offering Egypt its independence, the ties with the U.K. continued on all levels and in almost all respects. A significant privilege that the U.K. (and France) maintained was the administration of the Suez Canal that runs from Port-Said on the Mediterranean at the north to Suez on the Red Sea to the south. The fees collected from ships passing through the Canal were the property of the British and French administration.

In 1956, however, the U.K., France and Israeli forces attacked Egypt. The Israeli army moved onto the Sinai desert and reached the eastern bank of the Suez Canal. The British and French navy in the Mediterranean blockaded the Suez Canal. But the late President Eisenhower did not like what was happening, and, in a clear firm statement, ordered the three countries to back down.

Nasser nationalized the Suez Canal. Egyptian pilots took control of guiding the ships through the waterway. Egypt collected the fees to cover its dire need for foreign currency.

Some coming events, however, did not have such a happy ending. One of the projects Egypt had long envisioned was building the Aswan High Dam. Basically an agrarian country with limited natural physical resources, the country aspired to build a large dam at Aswan (the southern part of Egypt) as an efficient way to increase the area of farmland as well as using the dam to generate electrical power—an essential ingredient for the industrialization of the country. It had been reported in the media that the Aswan High Dam project had been thought about long before the 1952 revolution. But nothing was done to put such plans into existence. Nasser adopted the project. But Egypt did not have the money or expertise to handle such an ambitious undertaking.

Soliciting outside help, Nasser held great hopes on the U.S. But Milton Eisenhower correctly believed the dam would have more adverse effects than benefits. Egypt's request for funding was denied. This was an embarrassing moment for a rather young, ambitious and strong leader such as Nasser to accept. He had not much choice but to look at the, then, other superpower: the Soviet Union.

It might be appropriate here to interrupt the chronological sequence of events to look at the status of Nasser as a leader not only of Egypt but also as a leader of the Arab nations.

A natural leader, Nasser had all the ingredients of a powerful president. He had this ability that once he started delivering a speech one can not help but listen—even if you do not agree or like what he is saying. Without much effort Nasser could mobilize the masses in Egypt and many Arab states.

He strongly believed that if the Arab countries could come together their collective resources would allow them great leverage. While the masses were mostly supportive of Nasser's call, the other Arab leaders felt threatened.

The union between Egypt and Syria to form the United Arab Republic in the early 1960s was expected to be the first step in forming a coalition of Arab nations. However, the union lasted less than a couple of years and ended up on a sour note that left a bitter taste on the relations between the two countries ever since.

Shortly thereafter, the Egyptian army was dragged into a long, exhaustive battle in Yemen. The Yemenis wanted a unity with Egypt's Nasser but their rulers opposed the idea. Sufficiently far from Egypt, this war was costly both in human as well as in financial resources. The goal of establishing some coalition with Yemen never materialized, and Egypt wasted a considerable share of its limited resources (Egypt was never an oil-exporting country; it produces just enough oil to cover its domestic consumption of about 700,000 barrels a day). The Egyptian economy suffered gravely. The infrastructure collapsed.

As for the Aswan High Dam, Nasser extended his hand to the Soviet Union who, up to this point in history, had no presence in any shape or form in the Middle East region. The Russian leadership was quite responsive, and building the dam was soon underway.

This initiated a period of time when the gap widened between Egypt and the West in general. Cooperation with the Soviet Union grew to cover many areas from supplying weapons to trade, industrial projects, and providing scholarships for Egyptian graduate students to pursue studies for the Ph. D. degree.

And in June 1967 came the last straw. The six-day war ended in a disaster with the West supporting Israel. Egypt went through a very gloomy mood. Militarily there was defeat. The Egyptian army was deployed across the Sinai Peninsula. Israel bombed the runways in the airfield bases rendering ineffective the Egyptian fighter planes that became sitting ducks and suffered irreversible damage. The army field commanders started retreating, leaving their posts, and the soldiers followed suit. This demoralizing trajectory paralyzed the armed forces. The successive wars had an indelible cumulative effect on the economy.

Politically, Nasser was effectively ineffective. Roads, rail, transportation, and communication were extremely damaged to the point of nonexistence. To have a new phone line (no cellular phones at the time) one had to apply and wait for 10, 20, or 30 years. Public buses were overcrowded and in great need of maintenance. The electric power was usually interrupted, sometimes several times a day. All factories and corporations that existed before 1952 were nationalized with no compensation for those who founded such organizations. At the helm of these institutions, the new system (the revolution) valued loyalty over efficiency and qualifications.

To illustrate, military generals with no industrial experience were given the chief executive officer (CEO) positions in industrial ventures. At one point, the position of head of the National Research Center (NRC) in Cairo was given to an army commander but fortunately this was soon rectified.

So, by the late 1960s, Egypt was defeated militarily, its economy was in shambles due to successive, failed wars. In addition, the nationalized corporations were run to the ground by inefficient CEOs who had neither the required expertise nor the feeling of ownership that fuels the private sector. Patronage and corruption proliferated. These decrepit industries did nothing but further drain the limited economic resources of the struggling nation. No one any longer felt the shared responsibility of citizenship. Everyone was on his own trying to benefit as much as possible from companies that were owned by nobody (only the tax payers) and run by executives whose only interest was to keep security under control and employing as many loyal relatives and friends as possible.

The modest industrial production went south, and exports suffered.

It must be remembered that immediately after the 1952 "revolution" all political parties were abolished and the free press became a sort of dinosaur. Opposition was nonexistent at least publicly. The powerful "Mukhabarat" kept strong wraps on the populace. It was extremely unwise during this period to talk or complain to anyone that you did not trust 100 percent. Security of the system was of the paramount importance. Obviously, there were no legitimate channels for the citizenship to express its views and vent its anger. Passivity prevailed. The feelings of helplessness, alienation, and other negative behavior were prevalent for some time after the war of June, 1967.

A completely different image erupted only six years later, in October 1973, when the Egyptian Armed Forces surprised the whole world by crossing a paramount obstacle (the Suez Canal) and penetrated the heavily fortified posts of Barleev line right on the eastern banks of the Canal.

The difference was primarily in the political leadership at the top. This was coupled with a sense of redemption on the side of the Armed Forces that felt deprived of a fair chance of fighting in the 1967 war. "In politics and in war, truth can be elusive; often all we can do is muddle through, trying to make the best of things," wrote Jon Meacham, former-editor, NEWSWEEK in the October 19, 2009 issue, p.7, in an article entitled "Let Generals Speak their Minds" about the war in Afghanistan.

The political and economic policies adopted by the system from the early 1950s till the end of the 1960s had serious and far reaching implications on the social fabric of the country. A wrecker can easily demolish a building in a couple of days but it takes a concerted effort by a number of skilled workers over a couple of years to build a building. Many of the policies enacted during that period did just that—it gradually generated a multitude of negative behaviors that still permeate the society.

Consider housing. Up to the 1950s, Egypt did not have a shortage in housing. Rents were subject to the market's supply and demand. Because there was always enough supply the landlord seldom forced a tenant to evacuate the premises except, naturally, in case the rent was not paid or some other serious violation of the socially accepted behavior.

Egypt always existed around the Nile River. The ancient historian Herodotus wrote: "Egypt is the gift of the Nile." The great majority of Egyptians live in Cairo, the capital, and Alexandria on the north tip of the country overlooking the Mediterranean. It is therefore appropriate to consider these two larger cities and the effect housing policies had on them. Smaller cities and villages may not have suffered quite as much as Cairo and Alexandria.

Because of the ever-increasing population and continued internal immigration to the big cities, high rises were common. This meant that for one landlord there might have been 10, 20, or 50 tenants. Politically, and to gain favor with the masses, new housing policies were enacted in the 1960s. Rent was fixed at the time of the new law, never to increase again regardless of inflation, or whatever reason. Also, the landlord could not force a tenant out so long as he paid the rent, even two or three months later. If the tenant so desires, s/he can pay the rent at the court instead of to the landlord. Furthermore, if the tenant dies, the son or daughter living with him "inherits" the apartment, and the landlord must sign a new lease for the "heir."

In effect, the tenant became the actual owner of the property with the power to inherit it to his/her descendants.

Unjust for the owners? No doubt; moreover, they had no legal recourse. Whereas inflation reached astronomical figures, sometimes 50 percent for an item overnight, the rent remained unchanged. Older people who owned a property as their only source of income were in a deepening hole.

Before moving to the united States, my parents owned a four-story building with eight units in Maadi—a suburb of Cairo. This was a nice neighborhood where a couple of embassies were located and where the majority of Westerners lived while working in Egypt. After the author's father, a physician, passed away in 1964, the property was the only source of income for my mother (I had graduated from college a few years earlier and my sister was married). The rent paid in the mid 1960s is still the same more than four decades later! During this period inflation increased several hundred folds.

Unfortunately, bad policies usually take some time for their negative impact to materialize. Because of the enacted laws governing housing, those who looked for an investment opportunity turned away from owning real estate. By the 1980s a serious shortage of new buildings haunted the country.

Young married couples have either to postpone their marriage or live with their parents for years till they are able to locate an apartment for rent. Because of the high demand, whenever a unit becomes available for rent, the landlord asked, illegally, for a large sum of money—this was considered a "compensation" for the cheap rent to be paid by the tenant. Such illegal activity became the norm.

A misguided policy had unintended consequences. Sadat and Mubarak administrations rectified the problem at least partly by allowing landlords of an existing property to set whatever monetary value they chose for an apartment that became available for rent.

For buildings built over the last two decades or so, the landlord sets the value of the rent and a new lease with a higher rent can be signed every year for a maximum of three years. The landlord has the right to regain the unit at the end of the lease period. Justice and logic are eventually being restored, but the overall housing business had become fraught with deception and outright thievery. The damage done by the wrong policies of the 1960s had a long-lasting negative effect.

Consider farmland ownership. In all of its history the Egyptians owned and cultivated the fertile land on the banks of the Nile River as well as the "delta" (the V-shaped land extending from Cairo where the Nile River branches into a network of canals and streams that flow northward to the Mediterranean).

Before the 1952 revolution, wealthy Egyptian families owned large parcels of land. They hired farmers to do the job. The farmer paid some money as a rent for the land and the crop was the farmer's to sell. Because the owners were wealthy, they could afford having the needed fertilizers and equipment to raise plentiful crops. Egypt never had to import wheat or rice or any of the basic crops.

With his disdain for the wealthy, and to appease the masses, Nasser "nationalized" the land—he confiscated all the farmland. The land was subdivided and every farmer was given five "feddans" (about three acres). The farmer was supposed to pay the rent for the owner.

But, in practice, and realizing how supportive was the government for the farmer at the expense of the owner, the farmer rarely paid his rent. The system, including the courts, were on the side of the "poor" farmer and against the greedy owners. The farmer had very limited resources, could not buy fertilizer, and agricultural production went downhill. The rules regarding land ownership were improvised. The main two goals were to deprive the rich of their wealth and, simultaneously, empowering the poor. The first goal was achieved whereas the second goal never worked out for the overall benefit.

Recently, Egypt, the fertile agricultural land, has had to import large amounts of wheat, rice, and other fundamental crops. The high hopes for the Aswan High Dam proved illusive. The High Dam had actually decreased fertility of the land as it kept many of the necessary ingredients from flowing north and instead being deposited south of the dam. The price of electric power went up instead of down. A hurried policy was implemented without sufficient study of probable consequences. More harm was done than good; the negative results lasted for quite some time and Egypt is still paying a high price. But, politically, it appeased the masses.

Because the government took control of all economic activities it followed that all college graduates became the government's responsibility to provide employment opportunities.

Over time, the executive branch and the public sector industry were overburdened with human power that became a drag. The socialistic system proved a failure in all aspects. Privately owned department stores that compared favorably with their counterparts in Europe were also nationalized by the government. They became public sector property.

The author remembers when at an early age, my parents took me shopping at some of these high-end stores. The level of service and cleanliness were superb. But how painful it was to go to any of these same stores after nationalization. The merchandise, the service and overall appearance was disappointing—most were in a shambles. Employees enjoyed the security of public service with not much interest in carrying out their jobs to any satisfactory level.

Along parallel lines the government, with good intentions, aspired to convert Egypt from an agrarian country to an industrialized one. Many factories were built almost simultaneously. Instead of improving some already existing industries, such as the textile industry, or establishing and expanding those related to agriculture for which Egypt either had gone a long way or would have a good chance of gaining a bigger share of the international market, the new administration sought to enter new areas for which the country had no prior experience whatsoever. No coherent plan existed.

Furthermore, these new factories, all under the public-sector control, were put under CEOs and CFOs who, yes, were loyal to the regime but otherwise had no credentials to run these institutions. There was what is called "a five-year plan" but the fact of the matter was that there was no thought given to integrate the new projects.

To illustrate. Egypt needed and built a factory of Iron and Steel. Another factory for cement production was also built to handle the future construction projects. Both of those factories were ambitious undertakings and thousands of workers were hired. Because of the shortage in housing (the results of wrong housing policies were becoming evident) the government built housing projects for the factory workers.

Both the Iron and Steel factory and the new cement factory were built south of Cairo, whereas the housing projects for workers were constructed north of Cairo with about 50 kilometers in between. The result was time lost in commuting and overwhelming a transportation system that was already dysfunctional. To protect the new industries from outside competition importation was stopped.

On the agricultural front, the big farms that raised poultry or cattle were gone. (Wrong policies of farmland ownership). Egypt had to import poultry, meat, wheat and basically most other necessities including cooking oil, sugar and soap. By the mid to late 1960s it was customary to see lines of citizens in front of public centers that sold such items.

A couple of our friends, just returned from the former West Germany where they got their Ph. D's., were saddened to see the country deteriorating in this way. The wife once cried as she reiterated the humiliations endured when policemen had to keep order.

In short, instead of converting the country from an agricultural society to an industrialized one, Egypt attained neither. The government retained a vise-like control over Egypt's economy.

Luckily, this sad period in Egypt's history did not last for long. Sadat's administration extended its hand to the West while simultaneously working on putting an end to all cooperation with the Soviet Union.

Militarily, Sadat ordered all forms of Soviet existence in Egypt be terminated. This also included the large number of Soviet military advisers. He opened up Egypt's economy and society to the Western world and brought market forces to bear, empowering new groups and gradually taking the government out of controlling the economy.

Then President Mubarak continued along the same lines. Domestically, however, dealing with the social outcomes was, and still continues to be, a challenge.

The socialistic policies of the 1950s and the 1960s had a clear message that was repeated over and over in the media: the rich are corrupt with no interest in the good of the country. Therefore the government was justified in confiscating their factories, land, and other property, even including their mansions and jewelery.

Even those upper-middle class citizens who owned real estate were harmed, though not as severely as the upper class. The middle class citizens that owned real estate escaped losing their property altogether, but were dragged systematically down because their income from renting was frozen whereas inflation soared uncontrollably.

Socially these trends had two seriously damaging effects. First, there developed a strong sense of hatred and animosity between the haves and have-nots. With a small pie to start with, the feelings flared up. The lessee hated the landlord and used every bit of the law to hurt him. Farmers rarely paid the rent for the land they farmed.

Authorities were ordered to side with the farmer in case the land owner complained. Eventually, all those who owned farms sold them for any price—something is better than nothing.

The second effect was the growing sensation that any appearance of luxury is synonymous with evil and corruption. Nice neighborhoods, clean roads, and even nicely-dressed people were looked upon suspiciously. The upper and upper-middle class kept a low profile, and many of them left the country. Social behavior lost all signs of grace and empathy. Distrust, hatred, and disrespect prevailed—and still do to this day.

In the author's opinion, such a social breakdown precluded Egypt from attaining the world status it deserves. The country has a wealth of talented and hard working people who aspire for a better environment, which they require to flourish. May I provide a proof?

Consider the successful, achieving Egyptians who moved to the United States. Dr. Zuwail got the Nobel Prize in chemistry in the late 1990s. Osama El-Baz, a geologist, was involved with NASA as a manager for one of its outer space projects. Many M.D.s, faculty professors, engineers, chemists and geologists contribute to the advancement and progress of this great country that had opened its doors for people from all over the world.

In the United States, the author obtained a U. S. Patent as well as a Fulbright scholarship from the State Department to teach chemistry in Oman—both in 2003 (see chapter 16).

The above-mentioned political developments that engulfed Egypt during the second half of the last century carried a heavy weight in shaping up the society's culture. The social and economic implications of policies adopted during part of this period (the 1950s and 1960s) strongly influenced the popular culture. Part IV discusses these interactions.

CHAPTER 3

EGYPT'S REGIONAL FOOTPRINTS

Despite the ambitious, but generally unsuccessful, policies adopted in Egypt during the 1950s and the 1960s, the country by virtue of its long history, location, population, intellect had, and continues to have, a profound effect on neighboring countries and the region in general.

Any Arabic-speaking country, from Morocco, Algeria, Tunisia, Libya to the west, to Saudi Arabia, Syria, Lebanon, Jordan, Iraq and the Emirates to the east could easily understand the Egyptian dialect. The opposite is not true. Though one language, Arabic has so many dialects that mutual understanding can be very awkward.

The author got a secondment from the Egyptian government to the Iraqi government to work as an associate professor of chemistry at Mosul university from 1974 till 1978. Prior to that the author never thought a language barrier would exist—Iraqis spoke Arabic. It turned out, though, that communication with the Iraqis was not that easy. Many words were intertwined with the local vocabulary—Turkish, Kurdish and Persian words were not uncommon. The local dialect contributed a temporary obstacle to other Egyptian colleagues as well.

Citizens of Arabic-speaking countries become familiar with the Egyptian dialect essentially through entertainment. Movies, plays and songs produced by Egyptian artists and composers were in great demand in the Arab world. Egypt had the lead in literature as well. Most Arabic-speaking people were familiar with novels and poem written by Egyptian authors.

As referred to earlier, Egypt was much involved in the education process of some neighboring countries. Before the huge discoveries of oil in the Middle East in the late 1940s and early 1950s, Egypt provided teachers, reading and writing material for Saudi Arabia, Kuwait and some Gulf States. (The most ancient and prominent Islamic institution in all the Islamic world is El-Azhar built more than a thousand years ago in Cairo. The location where the Holy family crossed the Nile to the western bank when Joseph and Mary fled with the "boy" from Herod the King had a church built on it). These were prosperous times for Egypt.

But political, economic and social changes on the regional and international scenes brought about some incremental, but unmistakable, forces. First, the successive wars of 1956, 1967, 1973 and the military engagement in Yemen in the 1960s exhausted Egypt's financial resources and delivered a strong blow to the country's prestige in the region. Second, and simultaneous with Egypt's demise, was the accumulation of petro dollars in Libya, Saudi Arabia, Iraq, Kuwait and Gulf States.

Scores of Egyptians had no choice but to seek employment in those nouveau-rich states—a situation that prevailed to this day. Most of these oil-rich countries confiscate passports of expatriates upon entering the country for work. Passports are held by authorities and delivered back only upon leaving the country, even after the official approval of departure. Think of a big prison with no bars.

Confiscating of passports is but one facet of a larger policy. Expatriates are looked down upon both by local authorities and citizenry. The media act as the conduit. During the four years of the author's work in Iraq (1974 till 1978), President Sadat surprised the world, including Arab leaders, by his trip to Israel's capital. The Iraqi media and citizens called it the "trip of shame." Egypt was called and treated as the traitor for the Arab cause.

So fighting and sacrificing human and financial resources for Palestine and the Palestinians from 1948 till 1973 was forgotten and effectively denied. Interestingly enough those who criticized Egypt had always stood on the side lines with zero contribution. It was mainly because of these wars that Egypt's economy collapsed. In most of the Arab world, the Egyptians were referred to as those who eat "foul and taamiah"; both are recipes of beans, the cheapest food ingredient. Talk about mistreatment.

The late President Sadat had been widely praised in the West for seeking peace. It is hard to tell whether the same held true in Egypt. Yes there was no uprising against the administration, but this does not necessarily mean that the masses approved his approach of reconciliation. The author believes, however, that the intelligentsia admired his policy. Egypt, with President Carter's great help, got back all of its land that was lost in the 1967 war.

Since the late 1970s the pan-Arabian ideology had greatly faded. The peace treaty with Israel signaled the beginning of an era when Egypt had finished paying more than its fair share of sacrifice for the "Arab cause." The country had suffered a great deal and it was time for rebuilding.

With substantial aid from the United States, Egypt went back to trying to rebuild its house. For almost three decades, the U. S. had contributed two billion dollars annually in aid—one billion dollars in economic aid and one billion dollars in military aid.

Gradually the infrastructure was back on track. New roads were built, especially around the capital, to ease the burden on the overcrowded Cairo. New sewer systems replaced the deteriorating ones. Transportation improved significantly. Public as well as private bus companies operate in the capital. The shortage in taxi service is over. Ground phone lines are abundant—several private companies sell cellular-phone service.

So, it may be fair to say that there is a tangible recovery. However, attempts by the government to ease overcrowding in the capital (about 20 million people) and limit the population growth were not highly successful. On the intangible side, the difficult circumstances under which the people had to live had its negative impact on social behavior.

Intermittent trips to Egypt in the 1990s and the 2000s by the author revealed an increasing level of anxiety especially among the educated upper-middle class. High and sometimes uncontrollable inflation depleted the purchasing power of salaried workers and retirees. This had been coupled with the high tide of extreme Islamism. To consider this phenomenon, however, we may need to look at some political developments that engulfed the region in the second half of the 20th century.

Lebanon used to have a majority of Christians. It was another bright spot in the region but the civil war that started in 1973 devastated the country. Many educated and well-to-do Lebanese left to the West—most of those moving out were Christians. Lebanon no more has a Christian majority.

In 1969, colonel Moammar El-Gaddafi, emboldened by Gamal Abd-El Nasser's usurpation of power in Egypt, did overthrow Idris El-Senousy, king of Libya. The new Libyan president admired Nasser greatly and the latter sometimes referred to Gaddafi as "my son." But after Nasser's death, Gaddafi deployed the Libyan army on the western borders of Egypt. He aspired to force a unity of Libya and Egypt with him as president! The show ended without an incident.

The author's cousin, a civil engineer, got a contract to work for a Libyan company. At the port of entry he presented his Egyptian passport to the Libyan authorities. As it is the case for all Egyptian passports, and identification cards, there is an entry for the religion. It showed Christian as his religion. The Libyan official insisted that there must be a mistake as there are no Christians in Egypt.

Although there are no definite figures, it is generally agreed upon that 10 to 15 percent of the Egyptians are Christians. This is quite a few to be ignored.

In 1979 the Shah of Iran was deposed and the Mullas took power. So over a short span of time the region had seen a gradual but unmistakable shift toward what is known now as the Islamic tide.

The failed attempt to assassinate Nasser in 1954 and the implication of the Muslim Brotherhood in the conspiracy signaled, at least temporarily, a hold on the activities of said organization. Many members fled or left Egypt. Saudi Arabia, where most of the Muslim shrines are located, was probably at the top of the list for those seeking asylum from "persecution." The oil-rich country did also provide a good place for job opportunities. Kuwait and the other Gulf States, and later Libya, Sudan and Yemen were also candidates.

The Saudi Royal family had always had good political and economic relationships with the United States. Domestically the Saudi government did not object to having Islamic organizations being socially active. Actually, and to maintain internal stability, those organizations got financial support from the government, with the implied understanding that such organizations stay away from the political scene.

Yet, some fanatics, even from the Royal family, did not condone having such strong ties with the infidels, let alone have them on the "sacred" soil of Saudi Arabia where most of the Islamic shrines exist. Ben Laden had a fallout with the Royal family and fled to Sudan before settling in Afghanistan. Ayman El-Zawahry, the Egyptian surgeon, joined him later as the second man for Al-Quaeda. El-Zawahry was jailed in Egypt, together with others, due to his involvement in the assassination of Sadat but was freed in response to a plea by the Saudi government.

After 9/11, the extremists reappeared in the Middle East as well as in South East Asia (Afghanistan and Pakistan). They executed a number of strikes in Saudi Arabia, Egypt, Iraq, Turkey and Indonesia. On p.35 of its October 5th, 2009 issue of NEWSWEEK an article by Sami Yousafzai and Ron Moreau report on stories told by six Taliban fighters to the magazine correspondent covering Afghanistan since 2001.

The six participating Taliban talk first about their fall soon after the 9/11 attacks. One of the six told Yousafzai :

> "We gave those camels [a derogatory Afghan term for Arabs] free run of our country, and they brought us face to face with disaster. We knew the Americans would attack us in revenge." Talking about the rebirth of the Taliban, another of the six said: "At first I didn't hear the Afghans talking about going back to fight. But the Arabs did, and they encouraged the Afghans . . . . not to give up . . . . then the Arabs started organizing some training camps . . . . made friends with Egyptians, Saudis, Libyans and Yemenis" who were fighting in

> Afghanistan. A third Taliban talked about the role of the Arabs "who taught us how to make an IED by . . . . , and how to pack plastic explosives . . . . There were 200 of us . . . . divided up into 10 groups. Each had two or three Arabs assigned to it as commanders and instructors."

Talking about the Taliban surge the NEWSWEEK article reported on this stage as one of the six Taliban says:

> "Arab and Iraqi mujahedin began visiting us, transferring the latest IED technology and suicide-bomber tactics they had learned in the Iraqi resistance . . . . The American invasion of Iraq was very positive for us. It distracted the United States from Afghanistan . . . . our resistance became more lethal . . . . By the beginning of 2005 the Taliban began targeted killings of police officers, government officials, spies and elders who were working with the Americans." Another Taliban said: "Those first groups crossing the border [between Afghanistan and Pakistan] were almost totally sponsored, organized and led by Arab mujahedin. The Afghan Taliban were weak and disorganized. But slowly the situation began to change. American operations that harassed villagers, bombings that killed civilians, and Karzai's corrupt police and officials were alienating villagers and turning them in our favor." Another said: " . . . . money was flowing from the Gulf to the Arabs."

One of the six further elaborated by saying:

> "I helped assassinate those people who had continued their contacts with the government and the Americans. I didn't want to kill, but I was determined to bring back our Islamic regime and get rid of the Americans and the traitors allied with them."

It has recently been reported, by Mark Hosenball in the October 26, 2009 issue of NEWSWEEK, that the No.3 rank in Al-Quaeda is now thought to be held by "Mustafa Al-Yazid, a veteran Egyptian jihadist and an Osama Ben Laden associate. Yazid, who had been active in Militant Egyptian student groups linked indirectly to the 1981 assassination of late President Sadat, was an early member of Al-Quaeda's "shura council," or board of directors.

It seems probable, then, that disgruntled Arabs took their cause from the Middle East to South East Asia. After 9/11 the Middle Eastern regimes that looked the other way or even sponsored extremists began to realize the danger imposed by such organizations. South East Asia provided an unexploited, fertile land for fanatics to take their "cause." As Defense Secretary Robert Gates said, in an October 2009 interview on CNN together with Secretary of State Hilary Clinton, "the region in now the most dangerous."

This state of affairs poses some questions to be pondered. How and why did the Arabs manage to persuade Afghans and Pakistanis to get involved in this "holy" war? What is the common denominator that ties Saudis, Yemenis, Egyptians, Libyans from the Middle East with Afghans and Pakistanis from South East Asia who are separated by more than a couple of thousand miles? It is not hard to tell that Jihad for Islam is, and will continue to be, the driving force.

Ravi Zacharias, the contemporary Christian apologist, explained it best in his Spring 2010 letter. Zacharias wrote:

> "Most people living in the West have little understanding of the world of Islam. We hear and see what is only superficially apparent . . . . What is the interplay between politics, law, doctrine, and culture in Islam? A former Muslim once said to me [Ravi]: Draw a dot in the middle of a circle: if the circle represents life, the dot will represent the faith of the average Christian. For the Muslim, however, the circle represents his or her faith and the dot represents life. This is the greatest difference between how a Christian and a Muslim live their faith."

But then another question springs to mind. Why now? What developments, if any, did occur on the regional or international scene during the second half of the 20th century that had caused such a movement? As mentioned earlier, the three religions did coexist peacefully in the Middle East (Egypt, Lebanon, Syria, Jordan, Palestine) during the first half of the century.

Could it be the establishment of a Jewish state in Palestine in 1948, first with the support of the U.K. then later the United States? Many in the Middle East regarded the process as a collaboration between Christians and Jews in the West against Islam, manifested by expelling Muslims from a land they lived on.

Every time an Arab nation, or a group of nations, tried to defend the rights of the Palestinians, they were clobbered by military, intelligence and political aid to Israel from the West. Desperate, Palestinian groups executed some misguided attacks that did more harm than good for their cause. The most comprehensive, accurate and unbiased account of Middle East developments was written by the 39th President Jimmy Carter (Palestine. Peace Not Apartheid. New York, N.Y.:Simon & Schuster, 2003).

This may not be surprising since his sustained efforts had undoubtedly provided the impetus for a breakthrough in the region's politics. Since the Camp David agreement in 1978, the Middle East had not seen a large-scale conflict. Optimistically, the region is moving slowly but surely towards peace.

Solving the Palestinian issue could effectively throw cold water on the call to jihad in the Middle East by groups such as Hamas, Hezballah, Muslim Brotherhood or the Taliban in Afghanistan and Pakistan who had mainly been brought into jihad by the Arabs.

In a recent article about the Middle East in TIME magazine (June 7, 2010), President Obama said that settlement of the Israeli-Palestinian issue should help "drying up the rising well" of recruiting jihadists. These few words go right to the heart of the problem. This is the starting point. Distractions are numerous. Dealing with the symptoms only prolongs the agony on both sides.

As a teenager growing up in the heart of the Middle East, the author had witnessed firsthand the developments that engulfed the region since 1948 (the establishment of Israel). Followers of the three religions lived in peace and harmony till the 1950s when the regional political arena had seen some severe, successive and indelible forces of change. Polarization along the lines of religion dawned first within a country like Egypt and grew over the years to characterize the region as a whole. The coming to power of Gaddafi in Libya (1960s) and the Mullahs in Iran (1970s) were watershed events that exacerbated the chasm between Islamic societies and the West (Christians and Jews).

It may not be surprising, though, that the region that had seen the beginning of the three religions had become so polarized about religion.

In his book: "Learning to Listen, Ready to Talk," New York, Lincoln, Shanghai: iUniverse, 2007, Dr. Harold Heie (see also Part III, Chapter 8, of this book) designates Chapter 21 to "Tragedy, Just War, and Peacemaking." On page 150, Heie states:

> " . . . . proposing some steps . . . . that could ameliorate the escalating threat of terrorism. It is my conviction the the U. S. government has not adequately acknowledged or addressed all of the root causes of terrorism. The common view is that the Islamic terrorists hate us because of our western lifestyles, our democratic freedoms, our intermingling of genders, our civil liberties, or our separation of church and state. There are elements of truth in this view. But, as has been provocatively elaborated in the book Imperial Hubris (written by Michael Scheuer, a former CIA agent who was anonymous at the time of publication), the primary reason they hate us may be because of our foreign policies that are destructive for many Muslims. But the U. S. government has chosen, for the most part, to ignore this line of reasoning. Examples of such destructive foreign policies include America's protection and support of corrupt and tyrannical Muslim governments and, in my estimation, an obvious imbalance in support of Israel in the Israeli/Palestinian

conflict . . . . Our war on terrorism will be endless unless we adequately address these root causes".

The events associated with the war in Iraq and Afghanistan prove the validity of Heie's proposals. Iraq is still a hotbed for fanatics tied up to Al-Quaeda who attacked a catholic church in Baghdad early in November of 2010 killing 68 people and injuring a hundred more. Simultaneously, the same Iraqi group threatened Christians in Egypt of similar attacks. On New Year's eve worshipers in Alexandria, Egypt were attacked after leaving mass in a Coptic Church. The dead were 21, and several others were wounded.

The war in Afghanistan (started in 2001) became the longest war America has ever encountered. The situation in Pakistan (another Muslim country) continues to be crucial and sensitive. Sympathizers with the fanatics pose a danger to the ruling authorities in any Muslim country from Pakistan to Saudi Arabia to Egypt to Tunis and Algeria.

One of the side effects that the Camp David agreement had established is the creation of a buffer state (Egypt) that can be trusted, at least partly, by both Israel and the Palestinians. Regardless of all of the vicious attacks on Egypt and its policy by other Arabs who always did nothing but sit on the fence, Egypt remained faithful to what is the legitimate rights of a people living in refugee camps under inhumane conditions—by any human standard.

Over the last several years Egypt had, and continues to, work hard to bring together fighting Palestinian factions to help peaceful negotiations between Israel and the Palestinians—a task that may seem simple till one realizes the varying allegations and ambitions of all the parties involved. Egypt had not abandoned the Palestinian cause, but is just following another path to attain the same goal.

Recently Iran, through its subsidiary of Hezballah, had tried to destabilize the regime in Egypt. Thanks for an efficient security apparatus in Egypt, the plan was a failure, as was reported in the media.

In summary, it may be fair to state that Egypt had both a positive and a negative regional footprint. The negative being the rise of the

Muslim Brotherhood and similar organizations such as El-Takfir and Al-Hegra. These groups did not only sabotage the country's tolerant social fabric but exerted their damaging impact on other countries as well. But at the end of the day, the positive role that Egypt had and continues to play regionally can not be denied.

Fareed Zakaria, the renowned foreign-affairs expert summed it well during a TV interview on January 31, 2011 when commenting on the "Crisis in Egypt," he said: "Egypt is the heart and soul of the Middle East."

PART II

MOVING TO THE UNITED STATES

CHAPTER 4

A DECISION TO BE MADE

The 1950s and the 1960s had brought to Egypt some major changes that dominated the social, economic and political aspects of the country. The deteriorating morale and infrastructure left but little hope of recovery. An ever-increasing population, mostly among the disadvantaged and uneducated, further complicated the situation. In low-income neighborhoods children and young adults literally filled the streets. Within a decade or two all these individuals would require education, jobs and houses.

Other developing countries face similar problems. But a proper political system could positively channel the human power to slowly build the country. China and India are good examples. Although the last 30 to 40 years had seen a number of desired developments in Egypt, some social features seem to be intractable.

Among these features is the absence of any awareness as to limiting the number of children per household. On the contrary, the illiterates believe that more children is both religiously correct and may even bring more fortune as the youngsters grow to adulthood. The lack of trust either between the citizens themselves or between the government and its citizens is another serious social ill. The time spent on religious activities, such as praying five times every day, preferably in a mosque, waste time that could otherwise be spent on production. [To illustrate: In the 1990s, old-time colleagues talked about a practice that became popular among some workers at the National Research Center (NRC). Shortly after 11 AM they leave their work to go for noon prayer, to return around 1 PM].

The author, and many others, believed that a favorable outcome would be unlikely—at least for the foreseeable future. Married and with three daughters I could not ignore a sense of worry and concern about their future. My responsibility as a parent kept nagging me to take some action to secure their lives.

In 1967, the United States government opened, for the first time, the door for immigrants from Egypt. Simultaneously, Canada and Australia did the same.

It was a golden opportunity. Our application for immigration to the United States was approved in 1968.

But this was only half of what needed to be done. The other half was to get the approval of the Egyptian authorities to allow me (and my family) to emigrate.

At the time, Ali Sabry was the Egyptian prime minister. He was well known for his strong socialistic policies and ideas. One such policy put into effect was to close the door of emigration to those wanting to leave the country if they happened to have post-graduate degrees. At the time, my wife had a Master's degree and I had already got the Ph. D., and consequently we were legally forbidden to emigrate.

Looking back at the regional political arena at this period in time, it seemed probable that by adopting such a policy the Egyptian government sought to deprive the West (U. S., Canada and Australia) from a potential human resource. The diplomatic relationship between Egypt and most Western countries was at its lowest point after the 1967 war. But by the same token, for the government to limit emigration implied its awareness of the low morale that dominated the citizenry, especially the highly educated, ambitious ones.

A secondary factor that may have influenced forbidding those with post-graduate degrees from emigrating out of Egypt was the educational policy prevailing at the times. Free education from kindergarten all the way to college was provided by the government. To put it differently, the society had invested considerably in having a college graduate who is expected to pay the country back as a productive citizen by paying taxes and contributing to the well-being of the whole.

But in an over populated country with an economy that had been drained both by wars and misguided policies, preventing those willing to leave did not seem to be a wise decision. The opposite might have had a better outcome for all parties concerned.

It is worth mentioning that limiting emigration as an official policy was abandoned by the later administration of the late President Sadat (who came to power after we had already emigrated; see chapter 6).

So, I ended up with an approval of the American authorities to emigrate, but could not get out of Egypt!

A few years later, and through my work at the National Research Center in Cairo, I got a scholarship from France. It was the long-awaited opportunity to get out of Egypt.

Before leaving Cairo in October 1970 and heading to Paris, I made a request at the American Embassy in Cairo to forward my immigration file to Paris. Once there, processing of the papers could be initiated and we (my family and I) could fly directly from Paris to the United States. This would circumvent the political obstacle of forbidding some Egyptians to emigrate.

My wife and I (no children yet—my wife was pregnant) flew from Cairo to Paris. We contacted the American Embassy in Paris where our immigration file had been forwarded from the American Embassy in Cairo. The Embassy started processing our application.

In the meantime, our first daughter, Heba, was born in Paris on December 12, 1970.

Living in Paris, as in any metropolitan city, required a lot of money. My scholarship was not very generous. Housing was very expensive. After having Heba, life became even more difficult. Our baby, like most other babies, cried at night (when else?). The landlord's wife, living upstairs, was not very happy with that—understandably so. We were repeatedly threatened with eviction if we could not manage to keep the baby from crying at night—easy to say, but the few-months-old baby could not understand?! (Heba is now a practicing physician in Wichita, KS. I should ask her about how to keep a baby content all the time so not to cry).

Late in March 1971 we received a letter from the American Embassy in Paris notifying us of a date for the health examination in the morning, then the interview, and the swearing of allegiance in the afternoon of same day. We left our room in the Paris suburb of Rueil Malmaison early in the morning to be at the Embassy by about 7:30 AM.

The three of us (now Heba is in the world) went through the medical examination and shortly after 10:00 AM we were through with our morning schedule. The next step was supposed to start after 1:00 PM and could possibly end by 5:00 PM according to the printed schedule mailed to us together with the cover letter specifying the date.

So, from about 6:00 to 10:00 AM Heba did not have a diaper change and was quite ready for one. We were sitting on a wooden pew in one of the big halls of the Embassy. With no one around, Dawlat decided to do the diaper change while having Heba on her back on a blanket placed on one of the pews.

By the time Dawlat and I were finishing taking care of Heba and her stuff, we were surprised to see an Embassy employee approaching us to say that because we have a baby with us we do not have to wait till the afternoon to start the interview process. After waiting for a few more minutes, we were allowed to meet those in charge to take care of the remaining steps. Long before noon we were finished, and left the Embassy on our way home.

Four decades have passed, but my wife and I still recall this incident. I do not think we will ever forget such an act of kindness. Many relatives and friends have heard us tell of this incident.

By May 1971, Dawlat had felt drained. Heba's crying at night and the nagging of the landlord and his wife had taken its toll on us.

A friend and colleague was going back to Egypt after the end of her scholarship. The lady kindly accepted taking Heba with her to Cairo where my sister and my mother were waiting for her at the airport.

Shortly afterwards a letter arrived from the American Embassy in Paris notifying us that our entry visas had arrived and we need to go to the Embassy with our photos for the very last step.

At this point, and with Heba back in Cairo, immigration to the United States had hit a road block or a dead end. The following month, the time of my scholarship came to an end and we returned back to Cairo.

I was not very happy about how this ended, but on the other hand could not see a lot of wisdom either in breaking the family apart or in forcing my wife to emigrate. The potential difficulties logically expected at the early stages of moving to another country and culture called for a united husband and wife both bent on persistence and success.

By June 1971 the three of us were back in Cairo. And life went on. We both resumed our jobs at the National Research Center and got busy conducting research. Dawlat resumed her work toward the Ph. D. degree. But the desire to leave the country and emigrate to the United States never left my mind.

A few years passed, and on March 14, 1973 we got our second daughter, Rasha (in Arabic her name means deer). She is now an environmental engineer (with a degree in chemical engineering) working for Kansas Department of Health and Environment.

In 1974 the author got a secondment from the Egyptian government to the Iraqi government to teach chemistry at Mosul University (in the north of Iraq). Such programs are common in the region. Universities in Arab countries such as Kuwait, Saudi Arabia, Libya, Iraq, and the Gulf States fill their needs for college professors from Egypt.

The applicants are screened by the advertising institution. The length of a secondment is usually up to four years after which the faculty member returns to his/her previous position in the Egyptian institution where s/he was originally employed. The years spent abroad count as seniority—as if those years were spent working in Egypt. Such an arrangement is possible since all of the participating institutions, whether in Egypt or the other Arab countries, were public organizations.

Needless to say, universities in these oil-rich countries pay a good salary that far exceeds what is paid by the Egyptian government. Every year the host institution evaluated the borrowed professor's performance and, if the host institution's need persisted, the contract was renewed for an additional scholastic year—for a maximum of four years.

My secondment continued for four years and, in 1978, I returned back to Cairo. With the savings from the four-year work in Iraq, the author thought that life in Egypt would be tolerable. Having some financial resources, it seemed, could obscure real social problems.

It did not take long for the author to realize that the problem is not simply financial.

By 1978 the author had already conducted and supervised research work that entitled him to apply for the job of research professor at the National Research Center (NRC). Later that year I was promoted to the highest career research job available at the NRC. The year before (1977) Dawlat was awarded the Ph. D. degree in physics—solid-state physics.

It sure felt satisfying that Dawlat had achieved the goal of attaining her doctorate degree, and for the author to be promoted to the position of research professor.

In the Summer of 1977, Dawlat and I left our two daughters, Heba and Rasha, with their grandmother while we traveled to Aachen, West Germany.

There we had some Egyptian friends studying for their Ph. D. degrees in engineering. With their help (Dawlat and I do not speak Germany and few Germans can or like to speak English), we managed to buy a nice Mercedes-Benz. On our way back to Egypt we drove the car through Austria then Venice, Italy, spending a few nights on the road. From Venice we took the boat to Alexandria, Egypt.

As the author reflects back on this period in our life, it appeared logical why family and friends could not see eye to eye my renewed determination to leave the country and emigrate to the United States. I heard it, in one form or the other, from several people asking: why do you want to leave? They would say: you live in your own property in one of the best suburbs of Cairo, you are driving a Mercedes, and both of you and your wife are holding prestigious positions that also pay handsomely.

To keep hearing this well-meaning advice did generate a lot of agony. Moving to another country is hard enough, let alone a society with a completely different culture like the United States. This also implied starting all over and looking for a job. At the time the author was approaching the critical age of 40.

Fortunately, though, I was not aware of the generally accepted norm that in the U. S. 40 demarcated the end of "youth" and vitality—significant ingredients of those seeking employment.

Many a night I could hardly sleep. If it was only for me and things did not work well then I could learn how to live with my own decision. But how about a wife and, at the time, two young daughters? Am I greedy, or simply ungrateful for the many blessings that God had bestowed on me?

Whatever the uncertainties associated with leaving Egypt and moving to the U. S., it seemed the right thing to do. [During recent visits to Egypt, many of those who tried to convince me otherwise expressed their approval by saying: you did the right thing.]

Early in 1979, and to re-initiate my application for immigration, I contacted the American Embassy in Cairo. It turned out that immigration laws allow a one-year period from granting an entry visa to the United States after which the petition was considered void.

The processing that took place while we were in Paris, France culminated in having the entry visa being issued in the early summer of 1971. That is, by the summer of 1972 the petition for immigration was nullified since we did not pursue the last step and chose instead to return back to Cairo. Now, early in 1979, we again arrived at a dead end.

A glimpse of hope materialized during 1979 through my brother-in-law (Dawlat's brother). He had emigrated earlier in the 1960s and settled down in Houston, Texas. In December 1979, he had petitioned the authorities for the immigration of his sister and her family.

In July 1980, our third daughter (Shahira, meaning famous or well-known) was born. She is now a lobbyist and director of marketing and communications for Kansas Agricultural Association, as well as four other associations.

A month later (August 1980), we were notified by the American Embassy in Cairo that our entry visa had arrived. After preparing some required documents we went through the medical examination. The interview was in October of 1980 and we were allowed till March 1981 (six months) to be in the United States.

CHAPTER 5

GETTING READY?

After obtaining the entry visa and having the paperwork processed, there followed a period that was both hectic and immensely agonizing. We were fast approaching the point of no return—if you will. Some irreversible actions had to be put into effect. That was not a time of reflection anymore. Decisive steps needed to be taken. It was now or never.

Family and friends continued to provide their well-meaning advice not to leave the country. Torn between what most people around me thought and my personal conviction, I endured many sleepless nights. The pressure mounted as the six-month period (from October 1980 till March 1981) rolled by. The turmoil had to end, one way or the other.

It may be appropriate here to outline some of the prevailing circumstances of the Egyptian society at that time. To be familiar with the dynamics associated with the living conditions in that environment is essential to realizing how crucial it is/was for someone to make the decision of leaving the country and move to another.

First concerning the children. Our two daughters (Heba and Rasha) were enrolled in a private, English school that was 300 feet from our home. Back then, to get a child enrolled in a private school, the parents need to apply for admission years before the child reaches the school age—preferably at the time of his/her birth! A waiting list would be the determining factor.

We were fortunate to have both of them enrolled. Once they leave their spot it would immediately be taken. If for any reason, say we were unsuccessful in our new country of residence, and we returned back to Cairo, the children would have to apply as new students and take their turn on the waiting list. This process could take a number of years.

Second were our jobs. In a country with limited economic resources and an economy that had already been drained both by wars and by misguided, even if sincere, policies, the job market was exceptionally tight. Leave your position and the chances of getting something similar are slim if nonexistent.

Third was our home. This was probably the least worrisome. We lived in our property and had some control over that. But again, it would be a waste to leave such a property vacant for a considerable length of time until we got settled in our new country of residence. To offer it for rent would entail losing it permanently.

At the time, government rules and regulations withheld all authority from the landlord and bestowed all the power on the tenant who had the right to live in the property till s/he passes away at which time the tenant's son or daughter automatically becomes the new tenant. That is, once a property was rented the tenant becomes the de facto landlord, but without any responsibility or obligation (other than the rent, of course).

Lastly was the furniture and the nice car we had just bought from Germany.

Unlike Americans, the Egyptians are not used to, nor can, for the most part, afford to trade-in their cars, sell home to buy a bigger, more expensive one, or throw away furniture, appliances and TVs that were in good condition simply because a newer product became available on the market. In other words, Egypt is not a consumer-oriented economy.

"Change" is certainly not the keyword that describes Egyptian behavior. This is true for almost all aspects of life—economically, politically and socially.

Irreversible actions such as leaving a job, vacating a residence, children leaving a spot in a private school, selling a car or furniture can have long-lasting implications. This comes on top of getting away from family and friends—to leave the familiar to the unfamiliar. But like everything else in life, there is a price to be paid for a worthwhile goal. If it were only a matter of paying a price with the outcome being guaranteed, then the choice would be easier to make.

In our case, the price was to be paid in advance and the outcome was hardly predictable. It could take some years to find out. There remains the possibility that a negative outcome would be the result. Some of those who had moved to the United States could not settle down in their new country of residence, and chose to return back to Egypt.

However, it was my belief that those who returned did not have enough persistence or seriousness in carrying out this endeavor. Obviously moving to a new environment is relatively easier at a younger age. Even the foreign accent can disappear quickly if the young man or lady is younger than 12 years old. The author found out that this to be true with our two older daughters (Heba and Rasha) who were 10 and seven years old when we arrived in the United States. Within a few months they had no accent whatsoever.

I came to know that later when an American colleague called me one evening at home and was surprised to know that one of our daughters had answered the phone. He told me that he thought we had some American friends visiting since he could not hear the Egyptian accent. This was probably within six months from March 1981—the month we arrived in the U. S.

The author was familiar with the fact that moving from one society to another got harder as one got older. At forty (the age when the author would first hit the American soil) I would be right at the threshold of being too old to be employed. My accent would be indelible, and adapting to a new set of social norms may not be that easy. A considerable deal of thinking, observing and working would fall on the author in order to be integrated into the American society.

These challenges, however, did not deter me. A cost-benefit analysis favored going ahead with the decision to proceed. At a certain crossroad, the finite human being has to decide whether s/he is willing to put his/her trust in the infinite sovereignty of God. To the best of my ability, I had thought and analyzed the advantages and disadvantages of what might lie ahead of us as a family in our new destination. Beyond that the author had no control.

This was not a closed-minded religious dogma, but a conscious decision. How and why such a proposition played out might be seen from the following incident.

During a hot summer day of 1979, I was on my way to visit a friend who lived in Cairo but owned a farm some miles south of the capital city. The winding country road was two lane and asphalt paved. It was July or August, and at around 3 PM the temperature was close to 100 degrees Fahrenheit, if not higher. The traffic was slow, and the 240 SE MBZ felt very stable even at about 75 miles per hour (no speed limits at the time).

Suddenly, and just after one of those bends the author saw oil that was spilled and covered the road from shoulder to shoulder. The spill extended for about a quarter of a mile ahead. I lost all control over the speeding vehicle.

Hitting the brakes at such a speed would have been disastrous. All I could do was to hold on tightly to the steering wheel and try to control the sliding car. Raising my eyes from the slippery road I saw a bus coming at a high speed in the opposite direction.

Unable to control the vehicle my mind raced to face the inevitable. The bus kept approaching at the same speed. In the last few seconds and just before the car and the bus collided head-on, the slipping vehicle moved toward the left shoulder. The coming bus hit the tip of the back bumper as the car slanted toward the far shoulder. The bus never stopped or slowed down.

How can one explain what happened? The author was riding an out-of-control, fast moving car floating on oil. An oncoming bus did not swerve or slow down. A head-on collision was highly probable. A speeding bus carrying forty passengers would have the upper hand if it collided with a car. Death or severe injury of the car driver would not be unexpected. Yet the author was unscathed. Not only was I uninjured, but even the damage to the vehicle was minor—not in the body but in the back bumper.

Was this by chance? Or was it the guardian angel who pushed the car from the path of the oncoming bus? The two possibilities were valid. For the author, it was God's intervention that kept him safe.

This episode left an indelible mark on my thoughts. It was quite encouraging to perceive the Divine power intervening in my life. The slight hesitation toward leaving Egypt, and moving to the United States, got less and less.

CHAPTER 6

AT CAIRO AIRPORT

The American Embassy in Cairo had all of our paperwork processed. It was the regular procedure that, for those emigrating to the United States from any country, the entry visa was not stamped on the foreign passport but instead had it, and other related documents, placed inside a large manila envelope. The envelope was sealed by the American authorities at the Embassy in Cairo to be carried out by the immigrant who delivers it at the port of entry at the United States.

This meant that our Egyptian passports carried no evidence that showed we were entitled to enter the United States. To prove our status we must show the sealed manila envelope stamped by the American authorities on the outside. Egyptian officials at the airports were made aware of the process.

It might be appropriate to further discuss this point. During the 1970s some Egyptians flew to the United States without having an entry visa. Being denied entry, the airline carrier had to return them to Egypt at the carrier's expense.

The carriers enacted a new policy that required any passenger to the U. S. to have an entry visa beforehand. This smelled trouble for us. The employee(s) at the airport counter would require the proof of eligibility to enter the United States. For us, the proof was in the manila envelope. But this in turn meant that we were emigrating. We did not have the approval of the Egyptian authorities to emigrate. The numerous preparations for the whole process could have been nullified in an instant. But it was a risk worth taking.

In the morning of March 4, 1981 my brother-in-law (my sister's husband) drove us to Cairo airport to take an Air France plane on our way to Houston, Texas, via Europe (Belgium).

To leave Egypt, the citizen must obtain an exit visa, but to emigrate one must have gotten the official approval on his/her emigration. This entailed getting quite a few documents in an arduous process that usually took a minimum of one full year probably two. Furthermore, and more crucial, was the fact that both of my wife and I had got post-graduate degrees. This rendered us "not-for-exportation." It was possible, however, to ask for a one-month vacation to spend it overseas.

So we did. We got approval from the National Research Center to spend a month abroad. This, however, did not mean that we can officially emigrate. Our Egyptian passports were stamped with an exit visa—not an emigration visa.

It was not hard to get approval from our jobs to spend some time overseas. It was understood that those who requested approval for a vacation abroad had other plans and, on many occasions, did not return back to Egypt. Someone leaving his position translated into a job vacancy becoming available. There were always many candidates waiting for such an opportunity. If those who were planning to leave and never return were Christians, the better. It provided an opportunity to get the country rid of some more Christians. Such was the tacit policy and it worked well—both ways.

The explicit policy of restricting post-graduates from emigration was ill-conceived. Egypt had, and continues to have, an abundance of highly qualified people whom the country could not accommodate. In the following years the policy was rescinded.

At the airport, the carrier's employee—an Egyptian gentleman in his late 20s or early 30s started processing our airline tickets. Our destination was Houston, Texas. He asked where is the entry visa to the United States? I explained that we will get an entry visa to the United States once we reached Belgium. The answer was that since our destination, as it appeared from the airline tickets, was the United States, we must have an entry visa.

At this critical moment the author had no choice but reaching into one of our carry-ons to retrieve the sealed manila envelope. Before I could completely remove the envelope from the bag, the gentleman at the carrier's counter signaled his approval and, simultaneously, gestured his awareness of our intention to emigrate. A heavy burden was instantly lifted off my heart.

During the few minutes this dear gentleman worked on our tickets, and having our luggage weighed, I was mesmerized. Questions crowded my mind. Why did this gentleman behave in such an understanding and friendly manner? A few feet behind him stood two uniformed policemen. All that he needed to do was to turn back and, without even moving, tell the officers that we have here a family emigrating to the United States without approval of the Egyptian authorities. That would be the end of the story. We would be back to our home that now lacked a lot of stuff that we had sold in preparation for our moving out of the country. We had sold our car, too. Emotionally it would have been devastating.

I was still contemplating what had just happened, and how easily and smoothly things went.

Suddenly I heard another employee of the same carrier (Air France) calling his colleague—the gentleman processing our tickets and luggage. He called him "Milad . . . do you . . . ." The key word here is "Milad." This name is one of these names used only by Christians. There are many other names given to Christians, and another group of names given only to Muslims. Some other names are not indicative, and used by both Christians and Muslims. In Egypt, the name may be a quasi indicator of the religious affiliation. This is crucial in a country essentially divided across the lines of religion.

It became evident, Milad, a Christian, sympathized with a Christian family trying to emigrate from Egypt. The Egyptian passports, as well as other forms of identification, show religion (Christian or Muslim) second only to the name. The author always had great doubts that a Muslim counterpart to Milad would have done the same. We would never know.

Here again, how could one explain having a Christian—only 10 to 15 percent of the population, there at the counter to process our tickets? This seemed against the odds: only one in every seven to 10 Egyptians was a Christian. Was this possibly by chance? The probability was low, but it could have been. There was no way to find out if one considers this incident in isolation of other occurrences.

To the author, I was becoming increasingly convinced that the Divine power was again in play. It first saved me from death or severe injury while driving a speeding car floating on oil on a hot summer day on a country road. At Cairo airport, it was as if God was saying: go ahead, "I will not fail thee nor forsake thee."

CHAPTER 7

MERE CHANCE OR DIVINE INTERVENTION

More than three decades has passed since we arrived at Houston, Texas, on March 4, 1981. On numerous occasions, that will be mentioned in the following chapters, He was unmistakably at work. Each incident, by itself, may or may not be attributed to God's intervention. But it was highly improbable that it was mere chance that a number of successive events would have had the positive outcome that we, as a family, encountered over the past 30 years—a long enough period that is fundamental to prove the hypothesis.

Statistically speaking, a single event is assigned a value to describe the probability of its occurrence. This value may be between zero (0.00) and one (1.00), or between one percent and a 100 percent. The higher the probability value, the higher are the odds that an event would occur.

A probability of 90 percent rain tomorrow translates into rain being highly probable and expected. It does not mean that rain is guaranteed but is highly likely. A 50 percent probability denotes an equal chance of rain or no rain.

A more specific example is a large pack of m & m candy. Let us assume there are six different colors of candy inside the pack. To randomly pull a certain color, say yellow, of candy out of the pack has 1/6 (0.167 or 16.7 percent) probability. In other words, there is a low probability that one could pull a certain, say yellow, piece of candy from the pack. The positive outcome, pulling a yellow piece from the pack, has a 0.167 or 16.7 percent probability of happening.

What are the chances (probability) that one would first randomly pull a yellow piece of candy then on the second pull, would also get a yellow piece? The probability of this to occur is 1/6 multiplied by 1/6, that is 1/36; expressed differently, the chance is 0.027889 or 2.7889 percent.

The positive outcome randomly picking up two yellow pieces one after the other, has a lower probability (2.7889 percent) as opposed to the single event of pulling one yellow piece (16.7 percent). As the number of events increased, the probability of a favorable outcome decreased dramatically as seen from the above consideration.

Randomly pulling three successive yellow pieces has a probability of 1/6 multiplied by 1/6 multiplied by 1/6 = 1/216 or 0.00463 or 0.463 percent.

One might say that in a real-life situation (single event) there are usually two possibilities: success (positive) or failure (negative). The probability of success is 50 percent (1/2). The probability of success in a subsequent situation would be ½ multiplied by ½ or ¼ (25 percent). For yet an additional occurrence, the chances of success would be ½ multiplied by ½ multiplied by ½ = 1/8 or 12.5 percent. Consider a fourth event and the probability of success drops to 1/16 or 6.25 percent.

So, even when there were only two possibilities (positive or negative) the probability of a positive outcome (success) decreased significantly as the number of events increased.

Over the rather long period of thirty years, the number of incidents that all family members had encountered were numerous and not easy to count. By merely considering the laws of statistics the probability of positive outcomes should not have been as considerable as it actually materialized. It was the hand of God—His love and mercy that guided and carried us through by people who appeared in our lives at the right time.

The above reference to success, or positive outcome, does not necessarily imply material prosperity. We did not amass millions of dollars or start a multi-million dollar business. My wife and I did not waste our resources. We lived wisely, tithed our income, and reasonably enjoyed the pleasures of life.

We put our three daughters in college and paid all of their tuitions and expenses. The only exception was when our eldest daughter, Heba, got in the medical school with its exuberant expenses. At the time we had our middle daughter, Rasha, at the college of engineering and we could not afford paying her tuition and, simultaneously, pay the medical school tuition for her older sister. We still contributed a monthly amount to help Heba pay her medical-school expenses. We all felt comfortable with the arrangement.

Our youngest daughter, Shahira, was more fortunate. By the time she got into college (1998), we already had her two older sisters out of college and on their own feet. Shahira did enjoy some extra privileges both because our financial burdens had been lighter and our income had increased.

When Shahira asked for more privileges, we used to remind her that her two older sisters could not attain the same because we simply could not afford it. But then she would say: "Is this my fault?" How can you respond to that logic except by granting her at least some of what she desired?

Our three daughters have been, and will continue to be, the center of our life. The small sacrifices that my wife and I had made along the way are dwarfed by the feelings of love and appreciation our daughters exhibit toward us. If the author had the option to repeat, I would have done the same.

If success meant joy and peace of mind, we, as a family, had attained success. If success meant to see your children happily married and pursuing fulfilling careers, then we had been successful. To raise law-abiding, productive and educated citizens, I believe, epitomizes success. (Please see also chapter 17.)

It is my deep conviction that whatever the parents would do to raise their children right, it is God's blessing that keep them safe and guide them onto the right path. We are so grateful that ours turned out the way they are. Each is happily married to a wonderful husband, and each has two children.

PART III

IN THE UNITED STATES

CHAPTER 8

THE FIRST JOB

We were met at Hobby International Airport in Houston by my brother-in-law (my wife's brother) and his family. We spent the first few weeks at their residence in northwest Houston, then moved to a nearby apartment. We enrolled Heba and Rasha (the older two daughters) in a grade school.

It was around Mid March, and the school year had about a couple of months before summer vacation. Heba and Rasha were enrolled in Egypt in the 5th and 3rd grades, respectively. Because they will study a different curriculum in a new environment, we asked them if they would like to be enrolled at the 4th and 2nd grades during the current school year, and move up to their respective grades the following year? This would allow them some time to get adjusted. But they both said no, we like to be enrolled at our actual grades. And we did.

Soon the author started working on a resume. The weakest point was that all of my references were from overseas. My brother-in-law served as a personal reference.

At 40 years of age, my chances of employment were not that great. The 1981 and 1982 years were not the best years for someone looking for a job, let alone a newcomer with an accent and an unfamiliar name. The newspapers were writing about the recession which was later classified as the worst since the Great Depression—it lasted 16 months.

Instead of sitting idle at home while mailing resumes, I located a part-time job at a fine department store (Joske's). It was a good opportunity to practice the English language as it is used in the daily life.

In Egypt the author studied English as a second language for seven years in school and four years of college where all instruction material were also in English. All text-books we used were in English, so were the M. S. and Ph. D. theses. But it soon became obvious that daily-life conversation was a lot different from scientific English books and journals. Many words were new to me. More crucial was the context in which the words were used.

The cultural factor painted each word accordingly. Just to illustrate: to describe a 300-pound person, one says s/he is heavy set. In Egypt, one would say s/he is fat. Although "fat" and "heavy set" convey the same meaning, it is culturally not acceptable to use "fat".

A newcomer is likely to make mistakes like this, but needs to be alert and observant to avoid repeating the same.

A newspaper had an article about an Indian (from India) gentleman who moved to the United States. He had two grown-up sons who helped their dad running a gas station in one of the big cities. After a few months, the number of customers had dropped significantly to the extent that the family had to sell the business at a loss.

It turned out that when a customer pulled in the gas station to fill his/her car, the son would say to the customer: "what do you want?" instead of "can I help you?" For the Indian fellow, he was simply asking the customer, but culturally his use of the English language, though correct, was not acceptable if not outright rude.

Such is the case for all who move to another society.

The author was not aware of the "invisible space" that Americans are careful not to violate. Back in Egypt, one usually gets near to the listener as a sign of friendship. Not in the American culture.

The weather in Houston was nice in March (when we arrived). In April it started to get warmer and by May it got hot and humid. To drive from the apartment to the department store was impossible without turning the air-condition on even for this one-mile trip. The heat and humidity were suffocating.

We were happy to be in the United States, but anxious about what the future might hold for us—as individuals and as a family.

Considering all the facts at the time—recession, education as well as references from overseas, and an age of 40 generated a sense of uncertainty and a bit of pessimism. Others who emigrated before us said they had sent a couple of hundred resumes. This kept me going and encouraged.

Temporary jobs such as a replacement for a faculty member who was on sabbatical leave seemed appropriate as they offered less competition. I mailed applications for quite a few vacancies.

One such application was to Northwestern College, Orange City, Iowa—a four-year college. Their advertisement fit my education and background. The summer days went slow as I checked the mail daily. Letters of apology kept coming.

Late in June I received a call from the Vice President and Academic Dean of Northwestern College. Graciously, he explained to me that it had been a busy summer but they will soon be working on selecting applicants for the sabbatical replacement vacancy they have for the coming school year.

A couple of weeks later I was invited for an interview. I arrived one afternoon at Sioux City, Iowa. The author had dinner with the college vice president, his wife, two senior faculty members and their wives. The second day started with a breakfast, then a visit with a number of faculty personnel.

From 10 to 12 noon, the author made a presentation about his research work that was published.

After lunch, I was shown around the campus and again had the opportunity of visiting with faculty and staff.

At around 4:00 PM I met with the college president who made it clear that this vacancy to which I am applying is only for one year, and there was no chance of extending the contract beyond the coming school year. The faculty member on sabbatical leave will be returning to his position.

A dinner reception was held at the vice president's house and several faculty members were invited, together with their wives. About 20 guests attended the reception.

The author spent the night in Orange City (a room had already been reserved). Early next morning, the vice president drove me to Sioux City to take the plane back to Houston.

By then it was late in July and our daughters would soon start their school. The college vice president was responsive, and extended me an offer that I happily accepted.

On August 15, we moved from Houston to Orange City, IA.

This small town had a population of about 5,000 including the approximately 1,000 college students.

Orange City, like Holland, Michigan, had about 99 percent of its residents originally from The Netherlands. Any resident from a country other than The Netherlands is considered an outsider. The vice president, a Norwegian, fit the definition of an outsider.

Every year, on a certain day in May, the city celebrates the Spring by a tulip festival. Volunteers wash the downtown streets wearing their wooden shoes. The festival parade passes through the busy city streets full of tourists who come to enjoy this unique tradition.

Well, the months from September 1981 till May 1982 extended a really cold "hand" for us (coming from a warm climate).

This was our first winter in the United States. Snow is something Egyptians only hear about or watch on the TV. Iowa is known to be cold in winter, and Orange City is located at the northwest corner of the state.

That particular winter, we were told, was exceptionally cold still. Snow started accumulating by about mid September and by the time it started melting, a fresh layer replenished it. The lawn was continuously covered with snow from mid September till about mid May. What a greeting!

Teaching went well, in general. However, culture came powerfully into play one afternoon in the chemistry laboratory.

The author had collected and graded the papers for one laboratory experiment. Before we start the new experiment, I distributed the papers by placing each graded paper on the bench at the spot assigned to the corresponding student. Each paper was placed, with the grade showing in red, facing up.

Once the students came in and saw the papers, the stares spread like a fire. They were completely unhappy and I was not sure why.

What made me wonder was that those who had got high grades were even more upset than the others. So it was not a matter of shame for exposing a poor grade. I later came to know that it was privacy that mattered.

In Egypt, students felt good when they got high grades, and even bragged about it. They only felt embarrassed if their peers found out about their low grade.

How different two cultures could ever be.

Another cultural feature was revealed during this early stage in our new society.

The private college, with a student body of about one thousand, prides itself on the friendly environment that embraces the students as well as the faculty members.

While conversing with a friendly faculty member in one of the hallways, I stood about one foot from him. The author was surprised, at the time, to see him stepping one or two steps away. I was not aware of the "invisible space." He probably thought this was an invasion of his privacy. There was no way for him to realize that it was a cultural phenomenon that I was not aware of.

In Egypt, close friends, especially from the same sex, sit or stand not far from one another.

Unawareness of cultural norms can be embarrassing in a way. But I wondered how or why the invisible space became the norm in one society and not in the other?

Egyptians live on a rather small area of the country concentrated mainly around the Nile River. People got used to feeling physically close to each other. This contrasted the vast area of the United States where people can easily get away from any location they feel crowded. The population density is so small. The whole State of Kansas has about two and a half million people—one neighborhood in Cairo has more.

But what about Northwestern College as an institution, and its vice president who selected an Egyptian to fill out a vacant faculty position to teach students who were almost exclusively Dutch attending a college built in an essentially Dutch city? The common thread was Christianity.

Northwestern college was a church-affiliated institution. With a Ph. D. degree in Mathematics from New York City, the vice president (and academic dean) who headed the search committee was, and still is, a devout Christian. At the time, however, such information was not available to the author.

After some years, Dr. Heie left his position at Northwestern College and moved back to the East Coast where he taught and worked as academic administrator at the King's College in New York then at Messiah College in Pennsylvania. He was a Senior Fellow at the Center for Christian Studies at Gordon College, Massachusetts, and the Council for Christian Colleges and Universities before he retired. In 2007, he authored the book "Learning to Listen, Ready to Talk."

I am still in touch with him. He is a man whose life exemplified Christianity—a man loved and respected by all of those who came to know him. God had blessed me by having my early path to cross his.

Under the circumstances, attaining the first job was the gate opener. Or it at least enhanced my future opportunities for securing other jobs.

Still the country was in recession by the summer of 1982 when my one-year, nonrenewable contract ended. But then, references from the United States were available. A serious obstacle had been removed.

During this early period in our new country the author often thought: if I were an employer, why would I risk employing a newcomer from overseas who had a foreign education and had no American references to check out with?

Alternatively, there were already other applicants who suffer none of such shortcomings.

Was this by chance? Could be.

But the trend was becoming more and more compelling and harder to ignore. The same Divine power that had protected me from death or injury while sliding on oil, and arranged a Christian gentleman to process our airline tickets at Cairo airport had worked another miracle by providing my first job in the United States.

From all places, the job was at a Christian organization, and the job offer was extended by a devout Christian. The author just can not help but connect the dots, without any preconceived bias.

Does this imply that every single detail was just wonderful? Far from that.

Negative behavior and comments, whether intentional or unintentional, conscious or subconscious were not in short supply.

This was not surprising since Orange City is a small town in the Midwest where exposure to other cultures or ethnicities was almost nonexistent.

The only non-Dutch family was one from Vietnam that was 100 percent supported by the church. Although our physical features carried no resemblance to those of the Vietnamese, we were sometimes confused to be the church-supported family.

The Egyptians are known for their hospitality and generosity. To get familiar with the American society, we occasionally invited families of faculty members over for dinner. Dawlat is a good cook and, at the time, a stay-home mom.

A feature of Egyptian hospitality is not to just offer food but to insist that the guest should try this or that. The habit is more pronounced in people from Upper Egypt—where my wife originally came from.

So, she did what she had grown up accustomed to.

But sitting in my chair the author began to notice that hosting Americans in this way did just the opposite. Showing hospitality in this manner conveyed the unintended message of forcing food on the guests, and some seemed even uncomfortable.

Dawlat and I discussed the subject and agreed to just offer the food.

A newcomer needs to be alert to cultural shifts and do the necessary adjustments.

There is no right way or wrong way in showing hospitality, or any other social behavior for that matter. It is what a society agrees upon as the proper way.

The most common question raised once we said we are Christians was: of which denomination? It was not enough to be a Christian.

This was not unexpected in a country like the United States where the majority are Christians, and the denominations help identify the groups within.

This contrasted the social environment in Egypt where the dividing line is being a Christian or a Muslim; all Muslims are Sunnis and Christians are 95 percent Coptic Orthodox. So, the unspoken question is whether someone is a Christian or a Muslim?

CHAPTER 9

AND THE WHEEL STARTED TO TURN

The start of the Spring semester of 1982 signaled the splitting of my time and effort between teaching and applying for the next job. From the beginning, the contract with Northwestern College was non-renewable; it was a sabbatical replacement and the faculty member on sabbatical leave lived most of his life in Orange City and was going to return to his position.

Towards the end of the spring semester I got an invitation for an interview at a state college in Missouri.

The interview went well, and an offer was extended from Missouri Southern State College—a four-year liberal arts college.

Again, this was a nonrenewable, one-year contract as a sabbatical replacement.

Under the circumstances, this was great news. The country was still or just coming out of the 1981 and 1982 recession, and my employment history in the United States was still at an early stage.

In 1982, the unemployment rate reached 10.8 percent—reported George F. Will in the January 25th, 2010 issue of NEWSWEEK, p. 15.

In August 1982, we moved from Orange City, Iowa to Joplin, Missouri.

The two older daughters (Heba and Rasha) had to move to a new school, new teachers, and make new friends. They were 11 and nine-years old. The youngest (two-years old, Shahira) stayed home with Dawlat who did not work since we moved to the United States.

Over time, Dawlat started feeling bored at home. She did not like to teach, and Joplin was not the big city that could offer research jobs in solid state physics.

Missouri Southern State College offered some computer classes that she could attend free since the author was a faculty member.

In hindsight, this turned out to be one of the best ideas. Dawlat took many computer programming classes in the years to come and had a new career.

Recall that she started taking computer classes in the 1982/1983 scholastic year. At the time, programming was done by FORTRAN or COBOL languages with punch cards using the 0 and 1 codes.

The use and application of computers was limited. Its promise was essentially in its capacity to handle complex mathematical processes, and Dawlat had her B. S. with two majors: Physics and Mathematics. This seemed a good match.

At the time, some newspaper articles started discussing the future of computers. Would they stop at this particular application as a research tool, or would it expand into other fields?

The questioning did not take long and the Silicon Valley was "born."

A career in computer programming turned out, later, to be a blessing of God. Dawlat took her first job as a programmer analyst in 1987 (after we moved to Topeka, Kansas). She got several promotions, and retired in 2003 as a senior programmer analyst.

Heba and Rasha (our two older daughters) attended a school and made new friends.

As for the author, this 1982/1983 scholastic year was not very successful.

One of the students told me that "students did not like me the moment I stepped into the class for the first time."

It did not help either that the author was one of those who believed no student is entitled to pass a course unless s/he put in the reasonable amount of effort.

One of my classes was General Chemistry. It was intended for non-chemistry majors. There was a prerequisite for the course—high-school chemistry.

However, it soon became obvious that most of those enrolled either did not fulfill this requirement, or had somehow passed high-school chemistry.

To pass high-school chemistry a student should have become familiar with the symbols used to designate the elements. Each element in the periodic table is assigned either a one or two letters that are always used when writing a chemical reaction or equation.

For example, sodium hydroxide (NaOH) reacts with hydrochloric acid (HCl) to give sodium chloride (NaCl) and water (H2O).

We express the chemical equation as:

$$NaOH + HCl - NaCl + H2O$$

For the above equation, Na represents sodium, O represents oxygen, H represents hydrogen and Cl for chlorine. The chemical symbols are the "names" that identify the elements. Although there are slightly more than one hundred elements known now, the ones that are commonly used in chemistry classes are less than 40.

There is no magical way to enable someone to become familiar with those chemical symbols. Memorization and hard work are the only options. But some expected that the professor would somehow enter these symbols into their minds. Better yet, allow them to pass the course without knowing them.

Human nature is the same. Instead of blaming ourselves, we tend to find an excuse so as to blame someone else for our inability. Some claimed my accent as the culprit.

As the author reflects back on this period of time, I find it interesting that a student told me that "students did not like me the moment I stepped into the class for the first time." The following incident might provide some insight.

In a Sunday school class, the leader was telling the attendees about an encounter between some residents of the southwest corner of Missouri—not far from Joplin.

One group from Joplin went to a neighboring town to discuss a project with them. The visiting group did not have any one with a German background. The town's people refused to make any meaningful discussion with the visitors.

If it was any consolation, I felt somewhat better. If some people around Joplin rejected those who were not of German descent, what chance does one from Egypt had?

People come to the United States from all parts of the world. As the most prosperous nation, it had always attracted many ambitious, productive and hard-working individuals. The coexistence of multiple ethnicities in the "salad bowl" bestows an indelible strength to the country.

As the world gets more and more connected through technology and trade, there will be an ever-increasing need for the input of those coming from other cultures. To deal effectively with another culture requires an "insider" knowledge available mainly to those who had lived there.

A case in point. The November 2nd, 2009, issue of NEWSWEEK had on pages 43 through 45 an article entitled: "The Dissident Who . . . . ," by Owen Matthews and Anna Nemtsova about Russia. Nemtsova's background had provided the in-depth understanding of the Russian culture.

Depending on how one looks at it, the different ethnicities can work for or against the welfare of the society. For Joplin and its surroundings, it sure had a negative impact. But again, this part of the country is not a real representation of the whole.

In any case, my contract with the college was for one year and Joplin, as a city, did not offer much. Its proximity to the Ozarks was a plus, though. We enjoyed several trips to the region.

The "Passion of the Christ" play had been a new experience as it was performed on an open theater.

The 1982/1983 scholastic year progressed without much fire works. As the spring semester of 1983 started, I began the application process—again.

Applications were submitted, and more applications were submitted.

Slowly the spring semester came to an end, and the summer began.

CHAPTER 10

THE LONGEST SUMMER

With the passage of the 1982/1983 school year, two factors came into play. First, I could dedicate more time looking and applying for jobs. And second, the tension started to build up.

As the time went by, the pressure kept mounting. A new scholastic year was about to start, and our oldest two daughters needed to enroll in a school. But where?

Shall we continue to live in Joplin, Missouri? The town, or small city, had but very limited employment opportunities for the author or for Dawlat.

Shall we move? But where to?

Early in July of 1983 we took a trip to Houston, Texas to see my brother-in-law and his family. At least we have Dawlat's brother there, and Houston offered a better hope for employment.

We looked for an apartment to rent, and paid a deposit for the month of August.

Went back to Joplin. The long summer days went slow. Sleep was an expensive "commodity" that became harder and harder to afford.

The author remembers going to bed to have some sleep only to wake up an hour later with my mind spinning.

The same question kept resonating in my head. Shall we stay in Joplin or move? Houston, a big city, was not tempting.

After living in Cairo for so many years the author was not very eager to live again in a big city. But at the time Houston offered the only logical choice. Maybe move there just for the kids to settle down in a school and then look for a job there.

Houston seemed to be the location but only by exclusion, not by choice.

It was during these hard times that the author felt helpless—but not hopeless.

More and more the author became aware of the fact that there is a limit to what a human being can do. Hard times or disasters, not if but when they come, either get one closer to God or bring a sense of rebellion against the Creator who could be blamed for the circumstances.

It is a decision every human being has to make at some point or the other. We have been created with the freedom to worship and believe in God or to deny Him.

Before moving to the United States, we used to go to church every Sunday. We knew the Word of God. But knowing the Word is only the beginning of a long journey toward trusting in Him.

It is through life experiences that we gradually develop our reliance on His providence. Talk about the "purifying power of pain" as Dr. Charles Stanley said in one of his godly sermons.

Thank God that I was born in a Christian family. And thank Him that we moved away from the false sense of security that we had back in Egypt where family and friends provided a hedge against the unknown.

In our new destination we had no one to rely on but God.

Unless we are faced with a situation that reveals our inadequacy, we tend to continue our self-reliance. The feeling that we can handle it. Once we reach the point of realizing our limitations, God, in His mercy and love, steps in.

Then again, the human being has the choice to think that the help came from God or it was just luck.

The summer of 1983 was a turning point in the walk with God. The author believes that it was during that summer that he became a true believer in God.

Sometime in July the author received a call from a gentleman in Kansas Department of Health and Environment (KDHE) inviting him for an interview.

The interview was conducted toward the end of July. In the first week of August, the author got an offer to work as a chemist at KDHE.

The author accepted the offer, and we moved to Topeka, Kansas by mid August.

Our daughters got enrolled in school, and did not miss a single day of schooling.

The author started the new job on August 17, 1983.

The long wait and suffering was amazingly over in two to three weeks. Children were enrolled in school, and the author had a job. This was more than I had ever thought of.

But the greatest reward was the beginning of my true trust in, and reliance on, God. To be sure, His care have been revealed on several occasions that extended over the years to come.

CHAPTER 11

TOPEKA, KANSAS

We moved to Topeka in August of 1983 and lived there till we retired early in September of 2006. It was a good place to raise a family that offered a good education and job security for the author first then for my wife, later.

As the capital of Kansas, Topeka has both the legislative branch as well as most of the Executive offices. With a population of about 125,000 it could be classified as a medium-size city.

It has close proximity to the metropolitan area of Kansas City, Kansas/Kansas City, Missouri with around one million people. Two main State universities—University of Kansas, KU, and Kansas State University, KSU, are within less of an hour drive east and west of the capital city, respectively.

August 17, 1983 was the author's first day as a chemist with Kansas Department of Health and Environment (KDHE), Office of Laboratories and Research.

Let me first mention that there was no research work carried out, and it is now called "Division of Health and Environment Laboratory." This new name more correctly reflects the mission of the "Lab."

In May of 1984 we bought our first home in the United States.

It was a brand new house that was on the market for a few months till the developer was advised to do two modifications: lower the price, and put a window in the finished area of the basement (because of tornadoes, the basement provided a safe shelter).

We saw the house the first day following executing the proposed changes.

Both Dawlat and I fell in love with the house once we stepped in. The daughters shared our own opinion.

But how did we chose the location to look for a house to buy? Here is the story.

After moving to Topeka, I had to find an insurance agent to insure our car. The place of work was a few miles south of Topeka. By the time I got out of the office and drove to Topeka, most agents would have closed for the day.

I could not take time off since the author had not accumulated vacation time yet.

I tried again several times but with no success. By 5 PM most offices were closed. Till one day the author found Mr. H. Y. in his office staying late.

During our conversation he mentioned Lake Sherwood neighborhood as a nice place to look for a house (he lived there).

We did, and lived in that house for 19 years till we went to Oman on a Fulbright scholarship.

The neighborhood had the best schools in Topeka. An added advantage was that the school district (Shawnee County #457) had school buses to transport high school students to and from school. It was the only school district in Topeka and vicinity that provided such transportation for high school students. Dawlat did not drive at the time and the author would have to drive children to school both ways.

My particular job at KDHE was to handle the "Breath Alcohol" program for the State of Kansas. The KDHE enforced rules and regulations enacted by the Kansas Legislature. The job was a multi-faceted one that involved some scientific applications together with administrative and legal aspects.

At the time there were about 30 Breath-Alcohol testing devices distributed allover the state. Law-enforcement personnel were responsible to do the actual testing. We at the "Lab" prepared and sent out the standard solutions that were to be used to calibrate each device at specified time intervals.

At the "Lab" the author did the training for those selected by their agencies to be certified by the state to carry out the breath-alcohol testing on suspected drunk drivers.

Each testing device must be checked by the author at least once a year to guarantee its function and accuracy.

The job description also included providing expert testimony in court in those cases where the test result was legally challenged. The way the author understood the job responsibilities was to provide a neutral, non-biased opinion regarding the test procedure and the test result. In other words, the KDHE representative helps the system to reach the truth regardless on which side it lies.

This, however, was not always politically correct and, as time progressed, had some negative implications—on the job.

My understanding of the job responsibilities may not have been the only issue beyond what transpired later over a two- or three-year period.

The author's supervisor, Mr. R. D., told me the following details while we were on our way to a law-enforcement agency during the first week on the job. He had kindly accompanied me to show the proper way of approaching the new job.

On the way, the author became aware of the fact that the Lab director (top executive) was opposed to the selection made by R. D. to offer me the job.

This was, and has been, a surprise to me. The Lab director had never seen me, or participated in the interview process.

When the director objected, R. D. threatened to take the matter to court saying that the author is the most qualified—the job required a B. S. degree in chemistry with preference for those with a masters (M. S.) degree. None of the other applicants had got an M. S. degree, let alone a doctorate (Ph. D.) degree.

At the time, the author's background and experience were essentially in research (23 years) and academia (six years). In such a career, a high degree of autonomy is natural and expected. The author handled his job at KDHE accordingly.

In the 1970s and early 1980s, drinking and driving were considered to be a personal right, just like owning a gun.

But with the rise in human fatalities due to drunk driving, the government started a national campaign against such behavior. Each state enacted new rules and regulations to curb human tragedies.

Manufacturers came out with simple devices that can be used by law-enforcement personnel to test suspected drivers. But since the field was rather new, some of the devices sold to law-enforcement agencies were not fool-proof (a trend that was soon reversed).

In other words, some devices allowed the operator to set the test result arbitrarily.

In the state of Kansas, we had two (out of 30) such devices that were located in metropolitan areas.

Although there was a very slim chance that a licensed operator would tamper with the breath-alcohol test result, the possibility offered itself. This idea was behind having all manufacturers shifting the production to fool-proof equipment.

In the meantime, the author felt it was his responsibility to do something about these two devices. However, I could not figure out how to approach the problem. I was told that KDHE can not force a law-enforcement agency to buy a specific device since each agency pays for the equipment from its own budget.

But could KDHE take an action of not renewing the certification of such devices? At the time, a new fool-proof device cost about three to five thousand dollars, depending on the manufacturer.

Apparently, the subject upset some at KDHE, and at the two law-enforcement agencies.

What really mattered was that these two devices were replaced by fool-proof ones.

It also became obvious that each of the roughly 30 law-enforcement agencies followed its own procedure as for handling a suspected driver. There was no uniform process to be followed.

In 1985, the author put down the details of such a procedure.

All agencies were to follow one and the same initial steps, but differ from each other only in the use of the particular device they already have.

All agencies possessing a device from manufacturer "A", have one and the same procedure to do; those devices from manufacturer "B" would be used according to one and the same steps by all agencies using such devices. And so on.

This, the author thought, should create some sort of conformity in this legal endeavor.

Politically, this was wrong. Law-enforcement agencies rejected someone telling them what to do, and stepping in "their turf." It did not matter much that conformity would enhance the ultimate goal of curbing drunk driving by generating more confidence in the testing process.

But at the time, the supervisor and supporter had left the agency to study law (we would meet again years later and he would, again, have a positive impact on my career; chapter 16).

Mr. R. D. was replaced by someone with no experience in breath-alcohol testing, but a lot of experience in appeasing the higher-ups. Things went down hill after that.

The Lab director, within his authority, moved the author from breath-alcohol testing to blood-alcohol testing.

The job involved running the blood-alcohol content on blood samples sent to KDHE by the law-enforcement officers. If the defense challenges the test result in court, the author goes to testify to the performance and accuracy of the test. Again, this program covered all of the State of Kansas.

It was not unusual to receive a subpoena to testify in court. Drive several hours to be on time for the trial, only to be told that it had been continued. A day lost on the road away from the laboratory meant more blood samples in queue for testing.

Feeling the dead-end road at KDHE, the author enrolled in the University of Kansas (KU) for a masters degree in Public administration (MPA). I finished five of the seven required courses with a GPA of 3.6.

In 1986, another state agency got custody of the Blood-Alcohol Testing Program.

Once again, the author was moved to another area: water testing.

It was quite depressing to go through all this over such a short period of time.

Jon Meacham said it well in the article "Visions from a Vanishing World," NEWSWEEK, February 8, 2010, p.5: "Little is what it seems to be. The exterior appears solid and secure. But the interior is a constantly roiling emotional battlefield."

This quote well described how matters were at the time.

But God has His own way of letting us go through hard times so we may appreciate His loving hand as He open a wider door.

CHAPTER 12

MY WIFE'S NEW CAREER

Late in 1986, Kansas Department of Transportation advertised for the position of a research chemist. The author applied and got the job.

It was a great relief not only to leave KDHE but, more significantly, to get back to my favorite career in research.

On February 17, 1987 the author started the new job, and stayed there till retirement in September of 2006.

As known, a research job can consume 24 hours of the day. The author decided, then, not to continue with studies toward MPA—the only endeavor that was started and did not finish.

At about the same time Dawlat, feeling bored at home, got a job at a nursery as a baby sitter. She loved children, and enjoyed her job for more than a year.

Simultaneously, she got enrolled at Washburn University, Topeka, to study more classes in computer programming.

Together with the courses she took in Joplin, at Missouri Southern State College, she had a total of 21 semester credit hours—close to the requirement of 30 credit hours to major in computer programming.

Topeka, as a capital city, provided the opportunity to work for the state government. State jobs offer good benefits and job security—ingredients that were so valuable for our family at the time. We did need both of them.

Our daughters, Heba, Rasha and Shahira could enroll in schools and make long-time friends without worrying about having to move to another city and starting all over. They had gone through that as we moved from Houston, Texas to Orange City, Iowa, then to Joplin, Missouri over a period of just two years.

Thank God this was over.

One day my wife told me this story.

She had to renew her driver's license. At the time, the Shawnee County's office for driver's license renewal was located at the lobby of the State Office Building. This is a 12-story building in downtown Topeka. It hosted a number of State Department offices such as Department of Social and Rehabilitative Services (SRS), Department of Revenue, Department of Transportation and others.

Dawlat was early and had to wait for the office to open at 8:00AM.

While waiting in the lobby—not far from the six elevators, she saw state employees coming in for work and going up to their offices. She could not help but dream and long for a day when she could have a job with the state—just as those employees.

At the time, she had been working in a nursery for more than a year, and started to feel somewhat sorry for herself.

With all this education, baby sitting might be nice for a period of time, but as a career?

As it turned out later, God granted her that wish. But Dawlat did not spend much time complaining or blaming anybody. She did her part—enrolling in computer programming classes and applying for job openings until He opened the doors.

Dawlat applied for a job as a pharmacy technician. She got the job, and we were very pleased. The job was a part-time, but was a step better than working at a nursery, and offered a glimpse of hope toward career advancement.

Not long after that, Dawlat applied for an opening to work as a programmer II at Kansas Department of Social and Rehabilitative Services (SRS).

This was a big step forward since programmer I is the entry level for those without prior hands-on experience who are applying for such a career.

Well, on a Friday afternoon, Dawlat got a call from her would-be supervisor telling her that she had been offered the position!

To make certain that our hopes would not be dashed, the author went to SRS on Monday morning and verified there was no mistake, and that Dawlat had been selected by the interviewing committee to hold the position of programmer II.

How (not why) this happened became known to us shortly afterwards through Mrs. C (Dawlat's supervisor).

Mrs. C told Dawlat about the circumstances that led to the selection of my wife for the job opening.

Several months before, SRS had an opening for a programmer III position for which Mrs. C applied, and felt the most qualified for.

She was not selected. The thought of a civil service complaint crossed her mind.

Shortly afterwards, however, a similar job (programmer III) became available, and Mrs. C was selected to be a programmer III.

As a programmer III, a supervisory position, Mrs. C had a vacancy in her section. To interview applicants, the higher-ups formed an interview committee but Mrs. C, the future supervisor, was excluded from such a committee.

An outspoken person, Mrs. C objected strongly to denying her the opportunity to select the person with whom she would interact on a daily basis. Her request was granted.

She felt Dawlat was the most qualified, especially looking at my wife's education—a Ph. D. in physics, and 21 semester credit hours of computer programming.

The circumstances that opened the door before Dawlat for a long, rewarding career in computer programming were a bit unusual.

Was it just a random chance that sent Mrs. C our way, or was it the hand of the Almighty? The author have no doubt it was the latter!!

Here again, how can one ignore the outcome of previous situations : driving a fast-moving car sliding on oil, a Christian employee at the counter in Cairo airport, being selected for my first position to teach in a Church-affiliated Liberal Arts college by a Christian vice-president in a Dutch-dominated city, to be selected to work at KDHE at the opposition of the Lab director who opposed my selection based solely on my name, but gave in when threatened by a legal action by one of his subordinates who stood behind his decision.

Even the laws of statistics (probability) support a Divine intervention.

For one event, a favorable outcome may have a 50 percent chance. For two successive events, two favorable outcomes have a 25 percent chance, and for four successive events the chance of four favorable outcomes drops to 6.25 percent—a slim chance.

As the number of events increases, the probability of favorable outcomes decreases dramatically as was mathematically proven in chapter 7.

More events were still coming—all with the desired outcomes. This is what leads the author to believe that God's intervention could never be denied.

CHAPTER 13

BACK TO RESEARCH

With Dawlat starting a popular, and in demand, career, and our daughters secure from the anxieties associated with moving from one city to the other, the author was mentally able to concentrate on the new job of a research chemist.

Back in the preferred career of research, the incentive and motivation to go on with study towards a MPA degree quickly faded away.

The new job was a great opportunity to regain some sort of independence that is inherently associated with carrying out research. Obviously, some guidelines were in place.

Working for a State Department of Transportation (DOT) must fall in line with the agency's mission: to build safe and good roads that are part of the nation's interstate highway system. Roads are built using aggregates (different chemical compositions, shapes and sizes) that are held together using either cement (concrete roads) or asphalt (the residual byproduct of petroleum distillation). An additional material that is of concern to State DOTs is paint. Painted highway signs are exposed day and night to all weather conditions: heat, cold, wind, rain, freezing rain, and snow.

Every one of the 50 State DOTs has a well-equipped chemistry laboratory to test the chemical composition, and conformity of materials used for road building. Asphalt, cement, paint and steel are the most dominant. Tests are performed using standard test procedures mostly from the American Standards for Testing and Materials (ASTM). The American Association for State Highway and Transportation Officials (AASHTO) does provide standard tests as well.

Geologists study and examine rocks and aggregates used for road building. Chemists analyze and test asphalt, cement, paint and steel. Engineers design the roads and bridges. The three professional categories (geologists, chemists and engineers) share the same goal: well-built roads for the taxpayers.

In general, State DOTs follow the guidelines placed by the Federal Highway Administration (FHWA). A few State DOTs have research positions—mostly for engineers. Such research positions (when they exist) are scattered within the agency.

From among the 50 State DOTs, only Kansas DOT (KDOT) had a section totally devoted to research. The research section at KDOT has five research engineers, one research geologist and one research chemist—the position the author occupied from February 1987 till retirement in September 2006.

The fact that from all of the 50 States only KDOT had a research chemist position was quite a surprise.

The author came to know that by listening to some senior engineers discussing how other State DOTs approach relevant research projects. It just boggled my mind that the only research chemist position within the 50 State DOTs became vacant at the right time for the author to apply for. At the time, I was already working within the Kansas State system—and was ready to leave the dead-end road at KDHE.

The job vacancy at KDOT came at the right time when the author was at the right place.

After all these years, the author could not help but keep asking myself was this a coincidence? Or was it, once more, the Divine intervention?

Not only that such an opportunity came at the right time and at the right place, but it represented itself as one in a fifty chance. Let me elaborate.

As mentioned before, there was only one research chemist position—the one at KDOT; the other 49 State DOTs did not and do not have a comparable position. That is, there was one in 50, or two percent chance, to find a research chemist position within the 50 State DOTs. By any measure, this was a slim chance. Let us have a look at the laws of statistics.

Statistics usually deals with a large number of data or measurements. The bell-shaped curve of normal distribution is a fundamental concept upon which is based most of the statistical conclusions that can be inferred from a set of data.

The standard deviation is calculated by a simple mathematical equation, and is used to measure how far a given measurement is from the average of all the relevant data.

For example, for a set of 100 measurements, about two thirds of the values fall within one standard deviation; about 95 measurements fall within two standard deviations, and about all the 100 measurements fall within three standard deviations. Those five measurements (100 to 95) falling within three standard deviations are considered "unexpected," and there must be a reason that caused these five values to be that far off from the average.

Now consider the fact that from the 50 State DOTs only KDOT had a research chemist position (one in 50 or, for simplicity, two in a hundred). From the above discussion, the chance to find such a position falls within the "unexpected," and there must have been an unseen "power" that arranged for the author to be at the right place (Topeka, KS) at the right time (the position became vacant after retirement of my predecessor).

Some might argue that this was just good luck!

It seems hard for the author to believe that he had been so lucky to escape being killed driving my car over an oily, slippery country road back in Cairo, and lucky to have a Christian gentleman at the counter at Cairo airport that sympathized with a Christian family emigrating to the United States without approval of the Egyptian authorities, and lucky to get the first position in the United States in a church-affiliated college in a city of 99 percent Dutch Americans, and lucky to land the only research chemist position available in all State DOTs!! [If the author was that lucky, he might have won the lottery.]

In all of these circumstances, it was not the author's ability or planning that contributed positively to the outcome. Only the Divine intervention could have made it all possible. And how can the author fail to mention the circumstances that opened the way for Dawlat to start a new, successful career in computer programming—a career that she enjoyed till her retirement.

When the author joined KDOT, the Department had just purchased a new, expensive piece of equipment. The High Performance Liquid Chromatograph (HPLC) was still in boxes on the first day on the job. It was state-of-the-art that has recently been applied in research and industry to analyze a wide variety of materials. Asphalt, the final product remaining after petroleum distillation, was a candidate for study by HPLC. It was for this purpose that KDOT had bought the instrument.

The theory behind HPLC was not unfamiliar to the author. But he had never used the delicate, sophisticated equipment before. It was so involved that the manufacturer included in the price the expenses associated with two days of training for a person at their headquarters in Massachusetts.

Most analytical equipment can be used by following a set of defined, successive steps. Not the HPLC.

Several variables are available, and the researcher or chemist operating the instrument must set each variable so as to fit the particular application.

If this was not enough, the author's previous experience with asphalt was practically nonexistent (the same was true for the other materials of interest to KDOT—namely cement and paint).

Well, it became obvious that the author will have his hands full in the new job. The studies for a Masters degree in Public Administration (MPA) had to be abandoned. Out of 30 credit hours (10 courses) needed, the author had already passed seven courses (21 credit hours) with a GPA of 3.6. It was not an easy decision not to continue, but the challenges ahead favored a total commitment to the new responsibilities as a researcher. Study for the MPA was probably the only project that the author started but did not carry through. Anyways, getting back to research was a fulfilling enough reward.

There were other factors that favored the decision not to pursue the MPA.

The author was in a new job, and the administration at KDOT had high expectations for using the HPLC equipment to "solve" the problems associated with the different supplies of asphalt. There are no specifications for asphalt as a commercial material. Different refineries produce different qualities of asphalt. State DOTs do the best they can to select the best quality—that is, the one that is durable in the field.

A subtle yet significant consideration was the fact that the author was looked at as a "foreigner." Yes, he was a naturalized American citizen, but the name, accent and appearance tell of a newcomer to the society. Being under the microscope generates the feeling that one has to prove himself—repeatedly.

Does the feeling of having to prove oneself bring about a negative impact? I do not think so. It actually motivates, rather than frustrates. Many believe the influx of educated, experienced and motivated professionals helps sustain the status of America as the most advanced, prosperous and innovative superpower. Competing in the global economic race poses some serious challenges—now and in the future.

As is always the case with research, one has to familiarize himself with what has already been done. Gradually, some ideas began to crystallize. The author's prior experience in analytical chemistry proved helpful in tackling some potential problems associated with asphalt, cement and concrete.

After about a year and a half on the job, the first manuscript of a research paper was ready for submission to the Transportation Research Record for publication. (This is the Journal of the Transportation Research Board, a part of the National Academy of Science, Washington, D.C.). On average the author published a paper every year, and in some years two papers could be published.

While working on one research project the author realized the need for some knowledge in statistics. Washburn University in Topeka had a strong curriculum in statistics. A three-credit-hour course proved invaluable. The author enjoyed studying statistics, and was happily surprised to get an "A" for the final grade (there were three "A"s in the class of 50 students).

CHAPTER 14

CULTURAL PHENOMENA AND HUMAN NATURE

The author's job as a research chemist at KDOT, started in February 1987, had a setting that was much different from his previous jobs whether domestically or abroad.

Firstly, there were no other research chemists in KDOT or in any of the other 49 States. With the ever-increasing developments in technology and applications, collaboration between researchers has become imperative. There existed the possibility of collaborating with other scientists in academia or research institutions. But this could hardly substitute for the direct one-to-one, daily exchange of knowledge and ideas.

Secondly, the research chemistry unit comprised an engineering technician position in addition to the research chemist. The engineering technician helps, and reports to, the research chemist. Note that the supervised employee is called an "engineering" technician even though s/he works in "chemistry." All technicians at KDOT are assigned as engineering technicians regardless of the job they are actually performing: geology, chemistry, engineering or drafting.

The engineering technician that worked with the author (Mr. B) has been at KDOT for more than 10 years. He felt a sense of seniority. Two other factors helped exacerbate the situation: the author was looked at as a "foreigner," and Mr. B felt the backing and support of other engineering technicians—as a group.

Though subtle, class action does exist. Technicians did not really like their supervisors: engineers, geologists or chemists. This was implicitly felt and explicitly demonstrated on a number of occasions with the author as well as other colleagues at KDOT.

Was this an isolated case? Probably not. If one watches closely parallel situations are not uncommon.

Talk with a nurse about the doctor s/he works with. The nurse feels that s/he knows as much as the doctor. Or consider the machine operator in a factory who is being supervised by a newly-hired engineer. The experienced operator has the conscious feeling that he should supervise the yet-inexperienced professional. The fact that the professional has the education background that enables him/her to quickly get a grasp of the involved concepts escapes the mind of the operator.

Does this phenomenon exists only in the United States? Certainly not. It is actually much less apparent in the U. S. as compared with other societies. What helps keep matters in check is that the supervised (say nurse, machine operator, ...) is well paid, and has the resources to live a decent comfortable life.

Unfortunately, this is not always the case in other societies—for example, Egypt. Animosity is a common place. It is exacerbated by a dwindling income and social turmoil.

So, in principle, class action seems to be universal. The difference between one society and the other is in the "degree" at which the phenomenon exhibits itself. This may lead to the conclusion that it is the human nature—everywhere. The conflict is but one facet of the historic, human struggle toward what is perceived as a peaceful, fair life.

Communism sought to establish a classless society. In its failed attempt at creating such a community, it overlooked some imperative human impulses: ambition and motivation. It is the author's opinion that the downfall of the Soviet empire was rooted in the assumption that people can perform devoid of hope and personal freedom.

Someone said that suppose, hypothetically, all the wealth has been distributed equally between human beings. After a year, some would have increased their share, while others would have to contend with a dwindling resource. People are created with different talents and traits.

Going back to the author's tenure at KDOT, the gentleman that worked with him (Mr. B) was transferred to another job.

Then a female engineering technician (Ms. Y) was hired in his place. She was divorced and had a daughter and a teen-age son. She told me that she came from a dysfunctional family. Her sister "takes" something from her house every time she comes to visit. But this was not all.

Ms. Y was smart. After attending the college of engineering for some three years, she had to drop out, and never completed her studies.

When her daughter was in high school an accident happened. The chemistry teacher was performing an experiment in the laboratory when the material in the test tube caught fire. The daughter was standing nearby (together with the other students). The small fire was extinguished quickly, and no damage was done.

Ms. Y, nevertheless, sued the school on behalf of her daughter. To avoid negative publicity, the school district settled the case for a small sum of money. This happened years before Ms. Y joined KDOT, and the author came to know of the fact from her personally.

Another occurrence helped set a pattern.

Ms. Y was driving a Dodge, V-8 full-conversion van popular in the 1970s and the 1980s. Low on gas, she pulled into a small gas station. Behind her, in the gas station, was a compact car. For some reason the compact car rear ended the big van.

Ms. Y sued the driver of the compact car for injury to her neck. Again, some settlement was worked out. I had a hard time visualizing how a compact car moving at about five miles/hour could hit a full-size van strongly enough to cause the van's driver neck injury. But again this was her story.

The author became aware of the two above incidents on separate occasions. While telling me about the details, Ms. Y had an expression of slyness that worried the author a lot. The upcoming events proved the point.

Oh. Before I go on, Ms. Y told me about her small business.

She rented a store in a nearby town known for its antique shops. There was no shortage of tourists. Ms. Y got her "antiques" from garage sales in Topeka. She got items sold for five or 10 cents at garage sales and took it to her store to be sold as "antique" for exuberant prices.

One day, without a warning, the author's boss told him that Ms. Y had filed an official complaint against him. She was accusing the author of sexual harassment. This was the "fashion" of the 1980s and, probably, the 1990s.

The administration took the appropriate steps in such circumstances. Ms. Y was assigned a physical location away from her desk, and given the opportunity to write down all the details pertaining to her complaint.

To be fair, the author was asked to document his part of the episode.

All of the relevant writings, from both sides, were then forwarded to the Personnel Division to handle the situation according to the rules and regulations. At the time, the person in charge was an African-American lady with a Ph. D. degree.

A meeting was arranged. The Deputy Bureau Chief, head of the research section, the Personnel representative, Ms. Y and myself attended.

Some questions were posed by the Personnel lady to the two of us. After probably more than an hour, the meeting was called to an end. Every one left the room except the Personnel representative who requested that Ms. Y stay. They both talked for 10 or 15 minutes after which Ms. Y left the room.

From this meeting as well as the documentation of Ms. Y and myself, the Personnel Division came to the conclusion that Ms. Y had some issues.

The author does not exactly recall the details of how Ms. Y left her job at KDOT. Most likely, she stopped coming to work for more than two weeks. Attempts to contact her were unsuccessful or unfruitful. The Department had to terminate her services.

As the author reflects back on the whole thing, I wonder if Ms. Y was hoping for a settlement from KDOT? This may not be unexpected considering her previous pattern. Or did she simply try to destroy a human being?

About 10 years later, the author accidentally saw her. She apologized saying: "I am sorry to have caused you a lot of pain."

What an experience that was!

It took several months to conclude this watershed event. The author lived in turmoil not knowing what the end result would be. Although there was no wrongdoing on his part, the author was not yet completely familiar with the system and how it works. What if the author was mistakingly accused of sexual harassment? Would he lose his job? What would the consequences be on his future career?

At the time, Dawlat was still trying to start a new career. If the author lost his job how the family was going to survive? Our eldest daughter had just graduated from high school and preparing to go to college. How can we pay for her college education?

It is through such hard times that we have nothing to draw upon other than God. We get closer to Him. He never forsakes us. Our reliance on Him, and His faithfulness, build and strengthen our faith. The prize far outweighs the hardship.

Faith aside, the sad part is that the author did not learn much from this experience. It is just how life goes. We can not control the circumstances—only our response to it. Knowing that God is in control provides the peace to keep us sane.

After the two, not very successful encounters, first with Mr. B then Ms. Y, the Lord sent the author a very smart and efficient helper that was a great asset to the work. She stayed in her capacity till the author retired in 2006.

Ethel Herr in the book entitled: "An Introduction to Christian Writing," 2nd ed. Surrey: UK, Highland Books, 1999, wrote: "If light were never fractured, there would be no rainbows. And, by the same measure, if our lives were never broken, we would never see the splendor of one another's humanity."

CHAPTER 15

ASPHALT FOR ROAD PAVING: DIFFICULTIES OR OPPORTUNITIES

During the almost 20-year tenure at KDOT, the author's research work dealt essentially with two areas: cement and asphalt (what else did you expect?). But the latter offered more allure due to some associated features.

Asphalt is the final product of distilling crude oil. Petroleum companies build refineries that subject petroleum to a sophisticated process of distillation. In essence, this process involves heating the crude (in the liquid form) under controlled temperature conditions, and collecting the successive products as they evolve at specified temperatures.

As the crude heats up, the products first collected (at relatively low temperatures) are volatile liquids such as aircraft fuel. As the temperature increases, heavier fractions evolve. Gasoline, as well as many other products, are produced and collected separately. Then we get heavy oils and waxes. And what eventually remains as undistilled residue is asphalt.

From the refineries point of view, asphalt is, correctly, the least profitable component of the distillation process of crude oil. It is the end product—what is left after getting all the much more valuable commercial materials.

The term crude oil actually encompasses a widely different set of materials. A crude oil from, say, California will have some characteristics that are distinct from a crude from Saudi Arabia. The density and sulfur content of the crude oil determines, to a large extent, its value.

The fact that crude oils differ from each other may not be surprising if we consider how petroleum is formed in the ground.

Organic matter (mostly algae and bacteria) buried deep under the earth's surface are subjected to high temperatures and pressures for thousands of years. These conditions, are believed, lead eventually to what is termed as crude oil.

Because the starting materials are not uniform, and the degree of temperature and pressure as well as the time period are all not uniform, the end product (crude oil) varies considerably in composition and properties.

In addition to that, each refinery has its own industrial technique of distilling the crude. Distillation usually involves the use of catalysts intended to enhance the process.

All these factors contribute significantly to the diversity in the quality of the resulting asphalt. This black and sticky stuff, known as asphalt, does not, then, refer to a common product. Apart from being black and sticky, they are completely different from each other.

Application of asphalt in the field (paving roads) introduces yet another variable. An asphalt-paved road in, say, Minnesota might last longer (or shorter) than a road in Texas using the same asphalt. The difference in field temperature can not be overlooked. This is true whether we consider the temperature variation on the seasonal or the daily scale.

Albeit such difficulties, asphalt is still in demand for paving roads. It is much cheaper than Portland cement. In the late 1980s the Federal government initiated a five-year program called SHRP (Strategic Highway Research Program).

SHRP led to a new set of specifications for asphalt. Polymers were used as additives to provide better elasticity for asphalt at wider ranges of field temperature. The portents of these new specifications were good. But the inclusion of polymers in the asphalt raised an economic question. Even at the level of three- to four-percent polymer, the asphalt price almost doubled. Did the benefit gained justify the cost increase? Time would tell.

The foregoing discussion reveals the controversy abounding about the use of asphalt as a road-paving material. Research in asphalt laboratory-testing and application is inviting.

Producers (oil companies) and consumers (basically the 50 state departments of transportation) should carry a battery of laboratory tests that helps predict the asphalt field performance.

To ensure uniformity between the 50 state DOTs, the Federal Highway Administration (FHWA) adopt these laboratory tests after a careful discussion and verification of research work carried out at the FHWA, universities, research institutions, oil companies and state DOTs.

The new set of specifications adopted by the FHWA in the 1990s, as a product of the SHRP program, recommended an "aging" process of the asphalt to be run in the laboratory.

This process takes two days to complete. Laboratory aging is supposed to simulate the field conditions over a period of seven to 10 years. That is, an asphalt that is aged in the laboratory would have more or less the same properties as if it were laid on the road for seven to 10 years.

Asphalt-paved roads are subjected to pressure (traffic loads) and the normal temperature variations. It is therefore highly desirable to have a laboratory test that subjects the "fresh" asphalt to laboratory conditions that would produce an "aged" asphalt material so that the aged product is further tested to see the effect of aging on asphalt properties and hence its field performance.

It has been widely held among all those involved in the asphalt business (production, consumption, research) that an aging test run at the laboratory would be a significant contribution to the selection of the proper asphalt material; that is, an asphalt that performs well on the long run under the specified field conditions of traffic load and regional temperature.

But the fact that the aging process required two days to run presented an economic obstacle.

Refineries (the asphalt producers) deal with tons and tons of asphalt. Before shipping to the users (state DOTs), the refinery has to age a sample and run the relevant tests on the aged material. To have those huge amounts of asphalt waiting for two days before testing would require that the refinery build huge storage tanks to hold the material in the meantime. This in turn would require getting approval of the Environmental Protection Agency—a process that is both time-consuming as well as expensive.

A rapid aging test that consumes hours, not days, is therefore a necessity that saves a lot of time and expense.

In a research staff meeting at KDOT, the conversation touched on reclaimed asphalt. A deteriorating asphalt-paved road has to be torn up. Instead of burying the old roadway materials in a landfill, some companies collect the discarded paved material and heat it long enough so that the asphalt melts down and is separated from the aggregate. The resulting asphalt is called reclaimed asphalt. The latter is "softened" by the addition of fresh, low-viscosity-grade asphalt.

The reclaiming process requires heating the mix (asphalt and aggregate) at high temperatures. As the heating temperature reaches about 130 degree centigrade, dense fumes are produced (from the asphalt) that may cause air pollution.

To deal with such problem a company in Texas built huge microwave ovens that can attain such high temperatures (more than 130 C) to heat the mix. The advantage of this approach was the absence of the harmful fumes that cause air pollution. Reclaimed asphalt could thus be produced without environmental consequences.

The author became aware of the use of microwave energy for reclaiming asphalt at about the same time when a lot of discontent abounded regarding the two-day aging test that has been lately developed (by SHRP researchers).

Refineries, in particular, were the most disenchanted. Some even claimed that asphalt production is becoming economically unattractive as the new aging test would burden them financially (building storage tanks). A degree of unease was evident.

The author's line of thought was: if microwave energy can affect heating asphalt-paved road material—the mix, why not use the same energy source to age fresh asphalt in the laboratory?

The author contacted the company in Texas and asked them if they have thought about such an approach? That is, to use microwave energy to age fresh asphalt in the laboratory? The answer was that they have tried this idea and it did not work.

This was no deterrent.

Using a household microwave unit, the author started working on small (few grams) asphalt samples. Two variables could be controlled on a household microwave unit: power level and time of treatment (heating).

A reference line (target) had to be established. This was achieved by subjecting a given fresh asphalt to the established two-day aging process, then testing the aged product to find out its viscosity.

A sample of the same fresh asphalt was treated in the microwave oven at a certain power level for a certain time. The viscosity of the microwave-aged product was measured and compared with the "target" value.

After conducting a lot of experiments, it was realized that microwave energy has the potential of simulating the two-day aging process but in a much shorter time frame. The portents were encouraging.

This conclusion was not surprising, however. It is known that heating of a substance can be achieved by two ways: conduction (oven, flame, hot plate) or microwave radiation. The mechanism of heating is different, and hence the capability of microwave radiation to bring about an equal amount of heat energy in a shorter time period than could conductive heating.

A problem inherent with the use of a household microwave unit for aging asphalt soon presented itself.

A household microwave unit does not have the capability of controlling the pressure under which the asphalt sample is kept during treatment (heating).

This is significant since microwave aging of an asphalt run at a place near sea level (a pressure of 760 millimeter of mercury) would yield results different from those obtained doing the same but at a location like Laramie, Wyoming that is located at a height of more than 7,000 feet above sea level. The pressure is a variable that needs to be controlled in order to attain uniform results regardless of the location. Controlling pressure is a condition to be satisfied so that the proposed approach would be suitable for all geographic destinations.

In any case, scientific microwave units are available and are designed to be able to control the pressure, temperature, and power level. Furthermore, they allow the continuous supply of a gas (air or oxygen) to be introduced into the vessels containing the asphalt samples during their treatment.

The "only" problem was their price. One scientific microwave unit costs about $20,000.00.

Trials to have KDOT pay for a unit were not successful. The engineer of research—the author's boss, viewed the suggestion as secondary to the mission of KDOT to build roads. Aging of asphalt was not an engineering issue. That may be true. But selecting the proper asphalt is an economic concern that encompasses all aspects: scientific, engineering and economic. A faster method to age asphalt binders would benefit all involved in the asphalt business: producers and consumers. As mentioned earlier, state DOTs (including KDOT) must carry out the aging test in the laboratory to verify the quality of the asphalt being provided by the producer who also should have done the same before shipping the product to the state DOT.

Anyway, things worked out in an unexpected way.

The research work the author did on aging asphalt using the household unit was presented at a couple of national conferences.

The timing was perfect. The two-day aging process (adopted by SHRP) caused a lot of turmoil among all those involved in the asphalt industry. Most were unhappy with the long time it takes to age an asphalt in the laboratory. Microwave aging presented a highly desirable alternative. It offered the potential of achieving comparable results but in a matter of hours not days.

For quite a long time, Western Research Institute (WRI) has been the major player in the field of asphalt science. Every year in July,

WRI holds an international conference on asphalt-related research. In its headquarters at Laramie, Wyoming a gathering of chemists, engineers, geologists and marketers present and discuss their latest research work on asphalt.

WRI had the lion's share of the main contract offered by the FHWA under the SHRP program. The author had the opportunity to present his work at the annual meetings held at WRI. The research on laboratory aging of asphalt binder using a household microwave unit attracted the attention of WRI's senior researchers.

Following an annual meeting, the senior research staff member at WRI talked privately with the author about the subject. He expressed the interest of WRI in sponsoring this research.

WRI was willing to pay for a scientific microwave unit that would be placed in the author's laboratory at KDOT.

Great news—the financial obstacle would no longer be a problem.

Needless to say, the author had never used a scientific microwave unit before (only the household one to make tea). Consulting some specialized catalogs and calling a number of manufacturers led the author to decide on a company in North Carolina that seemed to offer the most appropriate product to fit the intended application.

There was no way the author could investigate, view and use each product available on the market. All he could do was to meticulously read the relevant material and discuss the goal with the manufacturers.

Up to a point, the author felt comfortable with the decision of selecting the company at North Carolina. The author is glad he did. The design of the unit they provided was well suited for the application, and the service they extended left nothing to be desired. Talk about God's guidance.

By controlling a number of variables, it was possible to age an asphalt binder in slightly more than a three-hour period. It took a couple of years, however, to establish the conditions of the "rapid" method for aging asphalt using microwave radiation (energy). This was judged from the fact that the aged asphalt product had viscoelastic properties that were practically equal to those obtained after applying the two-day procedure which relied on conductive heating.

Then came the idea of applying for a patent. Microwave energy has never been used before to age asphalt. The rapid method has the obvious advantages of saving money, time and energy.

The astonishing circumstances that surrounded the application for a patent will be discussed in chapter 16.

But two interesting phenomena became apparent over the years of involvement in asphalt research. For one, national conferences about asphalt were attended by, more or less, the same group of individuals. They represented a wide cross section of professions as well as employers. On one occasion a person worked, say, for the FHWA then in the following conference s/he would be listed as working for a company. The opposite did occur as well. The revolving door in operation.

Another feature that characterized the asphalt research "family" was "opinionatedness." Asphalt binder in the field is subjected to so many variables, some of which are hard or impossible to control. This opens the door to, sometimes, subjective arguments that can hardly be proved or disproved one way or the other.

Opinionated asphalt researchers are not an exception. As Jon Meacham, former-NEWSWEEK editor, wrote in one of his editorials: "faction is an inherent human impulse." This certainly adds more fuel to an already inflamed subject.

CHAPTER 16

A MEMORABLE YEAR (2003)

The 2003 year has been the year that the author like to think of as the epic of a career. In that year two watershed events took place.

The first event was the approval of the U.S. Patent and Trademark Office of the patent on aging asphalt by microwave radiation. The second event was the beginning of a Fulbright scholarship from the United States Department of State.

Let me start with the patent. The research work that have led to the award of the patent was carried out while the author was employed by KDOT.

So the first step was to discuss the idea of applying for a patent with the boss—the "engineer of research." A few days later he told me that application for a patent would cost KDOT several thousand dollars (seven to 10 thousand). He said that this is costly, and the administration was not interested in pursuing the matter—end of discussion.

Then one day, and under completely unexpected circumstances, the author came face to face with a patent attorney that turned things around.

How and where the author met Mr. R. D. is worth all the explanation.

Mr. R. D. was the supervisor in the first job the author took in Topeka, Kansas, in 1983. He was the one who selected the author, after the interview, to occupy the position of a chemist with Kansas Department of Health and Environment (KDHE). It was he who challenged the then-Director of the Office of Laboratories and Research over the said selection for the job.

When the author joined KDHE in 1983, Mr. R. D. already had a B. S. and an M. S. degree—both in chemistry. Smart and ambitious, he resigned his job at KDHE in 1984 to go to Law school (his conflict with his boss, the Office Director, probably favored the move).

As he told me later, he finished Law school and went to a major oil company to work as their patent attorney. He then did the same for another major oil company. He apparently had left his job as patent attorney when we met in 1999, more than fifteen years since we worked together at KDHE.

At that time (1999) Mr. R. D., just like the author, was teaching chemistry on a part-time basis at a community college (Highland Community College). The college had five different campuses spread across the northeastern part of the state of Kansas. Every year, the college holds a meeting for faculty and staff to get to meet and know others, and to discuss any possible topics that could enhance the college's mission of serving the community.

Because there are five college campuses, the administration leaves it open for faculty members to choose the geographic location of the meeting they go to.

It must be emphasized here that from the time Mr. R. D. left KDHE we lost contact. He had no idea where the author had been and, similarly, I had no idea where life had taken him. As it turned out, Mr. R. D. and the author had decided, independently, to go to the same location to attend the annual meeting!!

Was this just a random choice on part of the two persons? Maybe.

There is no way to prove, or disprove, that this was the case. For the author, however, it is hard to believe that out of five choices (five college campuses), two independent individuals decide to go to the same location. It is the author's conviction that Divine intervention was the driving force. What are the mere chances for that to happen?

Since we are talking about chance and probability, may be we should look at statistics—the field that deals primarily with probabilities.

For each of the two persons, there were five choices (the five campuses). So, the chance that a person (Mr. R. D.) choose site "A" to go to is 1/5. For the second person (the author), the chance to select site "A" is also 1/5.

Now, the chance that both Mr. R. D. and the author choose site "A" is 1/5 multiplied by 1/5 or 1/25, that is four percent.

Statisticians use the bell-shaped, normal distribution curve to look at probabilities of an event to occur.

The four percent probability (that both of us go to the same location) falls within the three-standard deviation region under the curve which, in turn, infers an occurrence that is unexpected, and calls for an explanation other than the usual and expected random distribution.

If we were dealing with experimental measurements, the explanation may lie with the method of measurement, the procedure followed to get the measurements, or the operator carrying out the measurements.

But in this particular situation, the event was influenced only by human choices, and the explanation, at least in the author's mind, is simply the sovereign God who is in control and guide our choices.

Back to the sequence of events. In the morning of the meeting, the author drove about 80 miles to the selected location. As I was entering the conference room, heard a voice saying: "Dr. Bishara."

Turning to see who was calling my name, it was Mr. R. D.

It was a great surprise and pleasant moment to see him after more than fifteen years. Here was the gentleman who had opened a door for me back in 1983—during the first few years of trying to establish a career in the United States. To meet Mr. R. D. again was enough to mark a special occasion.

The author did not realize at the moment that God had sent him in my way again to open yet another door by removing a serious obstacle.

During a recess of the meeting, Mr. R. D. told me about his prior experience as a patent attorney. After hearing a summary of what had expired about the work on asphalt aging, and the refusal of KDOT to pay for the patent application, he advised to go ahead with the patent. As for the employer (KDOT), the Department can always write me a "release" simply saying that she is not interested in submitting the patent. This would allow the author to submit the patent.

Elated, the first thing to do once again back at office was to talk to the boss.

Since KDOT is not interested in going ahead with the patent application, the author told him, give me a "release" and I will submit the patent and incur the associated expenses.

The author believes the engineer of research might have consulted with the higher-ups, and a few days later gave the O.K. to submit the patent. KDOT will cover all expenses.

Who said life was easy?

KDOT had already refused to pay for the patent application. Was it not for the information relayed from Mr. R. D. (who had worked before as a patent attorney), the patent would have never seen the light.

In the summer of 2001, the author submitted the manuscript of a patent written in the proper format. In June of 2003, the patent No. 6,571,648 was granted with the author's name as sole inventor (KDOT owns the rights to the patent as the employer).

The two-year period, elapsed from submitting the patent to its approval, was a consequence of the fact that the U. S. Patent and Trade Mark Office was understaffed. This was the subject of an article in the Topeka Capital-Journal.

May it be mentioned that the patent went smoothly through the review and evaluation process. No changes or revisions were required. The patent had been approved in its submitted form.

Amazingly, the author did not have the chance to thank, meet or hear again from Mr. R. D. Calling the phone number given to me by him got no answer.

Over fifteen years (from 1984 to 1999) our sole and unplanned meeting at the college conference was an isolated event engineered only by the Almighty!!

THE FULBRIGHT SCHOLARSHIP

For the author, getting a Fulbright scholarship has been a landmark in the career.

It is not easy to figure out which outweighs the other: a patent or a Fulbright scholarship?

But, then, why worry about an answer as the Lord, in His loving mercy, has chosen to offer His blessings with both gifts—and in one and the same year : 2003.

The developments that had led to getting a Fulbright scholarship appear to be worthwhile describing. This may be significant so as one might realize how our response to life circumstances could shape our destiny one way or the other.

May the author offer an invitation to explore how seemingly insignificant events could end up in a pleasantly major surprise.

In the 1998/1999 and 1999/2000 scholastic years, the author taught chemistry, on a part-time basis, at Highland Community College. The college campus (the one closest to Topeka where the author lived) was about 45 miles, one way, drive from home. This had to be done twice a week.

Then one day Washburn University in Topeka advertised about the need for adjunct faculty to teach chemistry. An application was mailed.

More than a month later, there was still no response. The author called the university. The call was transferred to the chairperson of the chemistry department. The time was about 10:00 or 10:30 AM—right in the middle of the busy morning. I expected to hear a recording saying: leave a message and we will get back to you as soon as possible.

But then came the surprise as the author heard the voice of the department's head on the other line.

The phone conversation lasted for more than half an hour. In hindsight, I came to realize that it was actually an interview.

Well, the author got the job.

Washburn University was a five-minute drive from KDOT (work place), and a ten-minute drive from home—rather than the 45-minute drive to Highland Community College. Not to mention that it was more rewarding to teach at a four-year university as opposed to a two-year college.

The chemistry department's chairperson was both an efficient administrator and a well qualified (a graduate of Johns Hopkins University) scientist.

The procedure was that each faculty member—including the adjunct ones, would have a pigeonhole for mail. This was a remarkable practice since adjunct faculty would not normally receive a lot of mail, nor they are expected to spend a lot of time on campus. But this was how it worked, and thank God for that.

Twice a week, whenever the author reached the chemistry department at the university I would check the mail box. Mostly was junk mail (what is new?).

One day in November 2001, the mail brought a few correspondence and a post card from some organization not quite familiar to the author. It was only minutes before the lecture to start. The thought came to mind to just discard the post card, together with the other pieces of junk mail.

Then it occurred to me why not keep this post card and look at it later on after having some time to carefully examine what it is about? The author inserted the post card in the brief case, delivered the three lectures, and went home.

A couple of days passed, and was about to forget about the post card. But as the author examined it more closely on the website provided, matters changed from reluctance to great interest.

The advertised program, in general, describes a number of scholarships available for applicants with various educational levels.

One of the programs involved seemed best fit for the author's education and experience. It had two deadlines every year: April and October. The closest deadline, then, was April 2002. This would probably allow enough time to get all the required documents ready.

As one would expect, the paperwork was quite involved and commensurate with the qualifications—it included:

A doctorate degree in the field.

A minimum of three years of college-teaching experience.

Publications in peer-reviewed scientific journals (periodicals). The applicant must submit a list of publications arranged from the most recent down.

A detailed description should be given for each course taught.

Three recommendation letters.

The 1040 Federal Tax Return for the last three years.

All this comes on top of a several-page, quite detailed application.

Before the April 2002 deadline, all required material were mailed to Washington, D. C.

Specialized committees in each discipline would handle the relevant applications.

A background security check is run by the State Department.

Letters of approval, if applicable, start to go out in December 2002.

This meant that the period from April to December 2002 would be a time of anticipation. And it was.

On the 3rd or 4th day of December came a letter—a one-page letter from the Fulbright Foundation.

Before opening said letter, the author recalled previous experience with letters holding one sheet of paper—usually a nice letter of apology.

Reality—whatever hard it may be, had to be faced.

Well, the author opened the letter, and was happily surprised.

The first word in the letter said: "Congratulations."

With great glee, the author read the letter that went on to provide details of the scholarship, and that I will be receiving forms for health examination that have to be taken to, and filled out by, my physician.

A clear statement in the letter warns against taking any irreversible steps, such as selling the house, since the final decision is yet to come depending on the health examination and acceptance by the host institution (where the Fulbright scholar would carry out his teaching responsibilities).

The health forms arrived by mail shortly afterwards, and there were no health problems (no surprises).

It may be appropriate to go back to the application that had already been submitted together with the other required material.

One of the application questions allows the applicant to choose a geographic location (a country) in which the scholarship would be executed.

Because of the author's Egyptian ancestors, it seemed a good idea to choose from among the Arabic-speaking countries. If I recall correctly, there were about ten such countries.

Some of these countries were excluded right away: Egypt, Syria, Saudi Arabia and Kuwait (the author had reasons for the exclusion). For those left, each country would get one scholarship from the Fulbright Foundation. Only Oman would be getting two scholarships.

At the time, this was enough to address the conundrum of selecting a country. Everything else seemed more or less equal, the probability of getting a scholarship would be doubled by selecting Oman.

And it did.

As one reflects back on this line of thinking, it is hard to keep myself from wondering how a minor observation or action could have such an indelible effect.

Selecting Oman proved to be one of the best choices the author could have ever made. But before explaining why, let us first follow the chronological sequence of events.

Once the health examination hurdle was taken care of, the last step was the acceptance by the host institution.

The United States Department of State designates scholarships to a large number of some specified countries, but in doing so, the Department does not force a scholar upon a country or an institution within that country.

The State Department contacts the institution and provides them information about the candidate. It is up to the host entity to accept or reject the person.

The Fulbright program does not object to, in fact it encourages, candidates to directly contact the host institution.

So the author got the E-mail address of the chairperson of the Chemistry Department at Sultan Qaboos University in Muscat,

Oman. A short message explained the interest in joining the Chemistry Department as a Fulbright scholar for the Fall semester of 2003—all parties involved were aware that all salaries and travel expenses would be incurred by the U. S. Department of State.

About three weeks later, the response came back. Graciously, the university welcomed the author.

Someone might wonder if the arduous task of applying for a Fulbright scholarship is a worthwhile undertaking?

You bet. It was worth every minute spent on it. How come?

Consider the mechanics of the program. Fulbright offers a specified (and generous) amount of money to be paid to the candidate here in the United States. The scholar notifies the program of a bank account into which the compensation would be deposited at previously set time intervals.

This process relieves the person of worrying about how, when or where the money would go.

More significant, the scholar would perform his/her teaching (and research) duties with the sense of being an honored guest—the obligation is to the United States as represented by the State Department and the Fulbright program.

The author can not help but contrast this feeling with the previous experience during the secondment from the Egyptian to the Iraqi government from 1974 till 1978. The person is completely under the control of the host authorities. They pay the salary, confiscate the passport and must give the permission for the faculty member to get out of the country—even during a vacation.

Talk about chagrin.

Going back to mechanics of the Fulbright program are some other distinct features.

The scholar has the option of taking the spouse and/or children with him overseas. The preset travel expenses are paid for by the program, depending on the number of family members traveling. A check is issued to the scholar who has the freedom to choose which airline and the best price available. The only condition is to use an American carrier. Fair enough. The author should also mention that the travel expenses received for my wife and I were more than enough (at the time, each of our three daughters was already married and had a job).

As if all of the above courtesy was not enough, the Fulbright program helps securing the entry visa—not an easy endeavor for most Middle-Eastern countries especially the oil-rich ones.

And we got it free for the two of us.

Obviously, each host country handles its entry visa differently. For the Fulbright scholar, Oman arranges it by having an Omani official, with the paperwork for the issued entry visa, present at the airport at the time of our arrival which has already been relayed to the Omani authorities.

We could not recognize him, but we were immediately approached by a gentleman wearing the national white "gallabia" and the characteristic head cover.

He asked for our passports, and we simply followed him as he proceeded from one employee to the other.

Within a few minutes all the formalities were taken care of. He returned our passports back to us, with the entry-visa stamp in place.

At the baggage claim area, we picked up our suit cases, and proceeded toward the exit. Not even a single suit case was checked by the customs. (It may be relevant to emphasize that our arrival to Oman was in August 2003, a few months after our forces attacked Iraq—not far from Oman).

During all this, the Omani official was ahead of us, and at the airport exit door, a full-size Toyota SUV was waiting—it carried the university's emblem.

The driver and the official loaded our luggage in the SUV, and we were driven to our on-campus residence.

The author had never before (or after) experienced royal treatment. But I tend to believe that what had transpired at the Omani airport in Muscat rightly describes what it entails.

Lodging in the host country of Oman was arranged according to an existing agreement between the Fulbright program and the Omani government. Lodging, quite expensive in Oman, was to be offered free to the scholar from the Omani authorities.

We were offered quite a spacious two-story, three bedroom, two and a half bathrooms single-family house on the university campus. It was quite comfortable, and probably more than what two individuals would need. It could have easily accommodated a family of five.

Oman, a Middle-Eastern country, was not far from Egypt; the latter was essentially on the way to the host country.

It has been more than 22 years since the author had seen the extended family in Cairo (the only exception was a short visit in 1989 to see my ailing mother before she passed away).

So, we planned our travel route so that we could spend two weeks in Cairo before flying to Oman.

It was a great opportunity to catch up with both of our families—to see the young ones grow up to become ladies and gentlemen. We can easily notice the time machine in action on others rather than on ourselves.

Dawlat and I (together with the extended family) spent a week at a resort on the Red Sea. Even though it was summer, we all had a great time together.

Then we flew from Cairo to Muscat—Oman's capital.

The author must admit that his background information about Oman was almost zero.

As a country, Oman did not engage in, or cause, any political upheaval in a region that has been engulfed by turmoil for more than half a century. It has been blessed by wise leaders who envisioned a prosperous future through building an efficient infrastructure. Oman has always kept close and friendly ties with countries in the region. More significant was its cooperation with the United States and the United Kingdom.

In contrast to the neighboring Gulf States (Saudi Arabia, Kuwait, Bahrain, Abu-Dhabi, Dubi), Oman does not sit on a lot of oil. Its resources are limited. But the Omanis are wisely using their resources. The last 30 or so years have seen an unmistakable progress that is evident from the new buildings and well-paved roads. The Sultan of Oman commands a genuine degree of encomium.

An obvious, striking feature of Muscat is cleanliness.

The author must admit to the fact that such cleanliness is not common to most Middle-East countries.

Consider Egypt as an example.

Egyptian homes are clean to the extreme. But city streets are another story. This is hard to reconcile for one and the same society, clean homes with anything-but clean streets. Well, may be this is one of the mysteries of Egypt.

An Egyptian journalist once commented on the phenomenon: Egyptians clean their homes and dump the trash outside. Their responsibility ends at the front door.

Could this be an indication of the lack of any obligation toward the community or the society as a whole? My home is clean, but the street is not my concern. In fact, authorities provide waste baskets, and trucks collect garbage, but dumping never eases nor stops.

Maybe this is why the author was pleasantly surprised to notice how clean Muscat was. All streets were meticulously clean. During the "Christmas" break—the period between the Fall and Spring semesters, the campus streets were successively closed to traffic in order to enable cleaning crews to scrub (yes, scrub) the pavement.

Expatriates, like ourselves, meet on some occasions to socialize. The author does recall hearing another patriot saying that Muscat has been selected as one of the most clean cities in the world. This was no surprise as we had already noticed by our own eyes. Keep in mind that the author had been to some European (Paris, Venice, Marcille) and Middle-Eastern (Cairo, Damascus, Amman, Kuwait, Baghdad, Mosul) cities. Only Aachen, Germany could come close.

Cleanliness was not restricted to the streets of Muscat.

As a college professor, the author had the opportunity of being in continuous contact with the students as representatives of a wide spectrum of the society as a whole.

All male students wear white "gallabia." Never once saw a student wearing a "gallabia" that was not as clean as it could be, and that was ironed to perfection. The same applied to female students who wore long, black dresses with their hair (not the face) covered.

Think of integration. It seems that rarely a phenomenon exists in isolation. Clean individuals would comfortably and naturally enjoy and maintain clean streets.

May I submit a hypothesis by extending the above observations a step further?

Wearing neat clothing and maintaining clean streets could be the outside expressions and portents of an innate national character. Omanis, in general, are decent, friendly and helpful people. Almost all expatriates agreed on this.

On two specific occasions the true nature of Omanis was manifested.

One night, my wife was riding with me on our way to visit some friends. At some point, the author, apparently, made a wrong turn. It did not take long to realize that we were lost.

The lights were turned on in one of the small businesses dotting the street. Got out of the car and went inside the shop to get some directions.

The owner (an Omani, by dress) said a few words to his assistant then turned to me and said: follow me. He got into his parked car and we followed him for a couple of miles before he pulled over and waived at the building we sought.

For a stranger lost at night in a foreign country, this action exceeded anyone's expectations. It has been itched in my memory.

Could this have been an isolated case where we just got lucky to solicit the help of the "right" person? Not so.

A few weeks later, the author was on his way to the American Embassy in Muscat to do some business. It was about 10:00 AM when it became obvious that the street I was driving on would lead nowhere (no maps for Muscat streets were available at the time).

On a curb, three or four Omani gentlemen in their twenties were chatting. Getting out of the car, the author asked them for directions. One of them signaled if I could wait a little so they could finish smoking their cigarettes. Then two of them jumped in a car and the author followed them. They drove until we arrived at the Embassy.

The two incidents left no doubt to be pondered.

It was not a matter of chance then, but the nature of the Omani people—friendly and helpful. Talking with other expatriates about what transpired, no one seemed surprised. Those who have been in Oman for some time had arrived at the same conclusion.

The author tends to believe this behavior is one of the reasons that endears Oman to expatriates.

Omanis are polite. A trait that is also true for college students. It was interesting to observe how male students treated each other, their female counterparts and the faculty. College professors who taught at universities in neighboring countries (Saudi Arabia, Kuwait, United Arab Emirates) told of how students behaved there. Their attitude conveyed a message: you are hired by us to teach us, so do it.

Not the Omani students. They were quite respectful.

To their credit, Omani students were smart and hard working. They have a great deal for lore. The lack of nighttime social life might have helped. I never noticed an impertinent act by any student whether in the classroom, laboratory or on campus.

As one would logically expect, not only students but Omanis in general are polite and courteous.

One evening, my wife and I were in a mall (not for shopping, but just to spend some time).

Standing not far from an elevator, the author noticed two separate groups of people approaching the escalator. One group were Indians, the other were Omanis in their twenties or thirties. The Omani group took a step back to allow the expatriates (the Indians) to step onto the escalator first.

Such graciousness was not uncommon. Other expatriates recounted other circumstances that led them to the same conclusion.

Like most Middle-Eastern countries (with the exception of Lebanon at least till the early 1970s), Oman is dominantly Muslims. But they follow the most simple and tolerant faction of Islam. The Ibadi sect is prominent in Oman.

A case in point is the call for prayer. Loudspeakers are mounted high on the "manaret" of mosques to announce the time of prayer—five times a day. Though loudspeakers are mounted, the author never recall for even once hearing the loud voice of the "Imam" calling for prayer. The university campus has an elegant mosque with loudspeakers. On the way to the chemistry department the author walks on the curb right in front of the mosque. Throughout my stay in Muscat, the call for prayer was never loud enough to be audible by pedestrians passing by the mosque (worshipers are expected to know the time of prayer on their own without the need for a loudspeaker to remind them).

One can not help but compare this phenomenon with what is going on in Egypt.

Loudspeakers are so loud to wake you up from deep sleep at dawn (around 3:30 or 4:00 AM). There is no escape from it—mosques are so abundant and are everywhere. Obviously, the call for prayer is still announced five times a day, but the most disturbing is the one that breaks the peace and quietness of dawn.

Such ostentatious practice of Islam in Egypt does not reflect a better society than, say, Oman. Actually, the opposite may be true.

Again, barely a phenomenon exists in isolation. The high tolerance of the Omanis ties well with the presence of several churches in Muscat—this is not the case in several neighboring countries.

My wife and I attended a nondenominational Protestant church. The land upon which the church was built had been donated by Sultan Qaboos himself. Now if this seems trivial consider the neighboring countries of Saudi Arabia and Kuwait. No churches ever existed. Not only that, but Bibles are not allowed in these countries. If the customs found a Bible in your luggage on entry, they confiscate it and probably deny you an entry. Such is the contrast between Oman and its neighboring countries.

Oman distinguished itself from neighboring countries in another aspect.

Ladies walk and drive by themselves. Female employees work everywhere—in banks, private companies, government offices and department stores. They wear long black dresses and cover their hair but not their faces.

A special event that continues to endear to memory our stay in Oman is the reception held by the United States Embassy in Muscat in honor of the two Fulbright scholars.

Sometime in September 2003, a special invitation was hand delivered to the university (no postage stamps). The author found a nice envelope in my pigeonhole at the chemistry department.

The other Fulbright scholar, his wife, my wife and I drove to the specified location. The area around the building was surrounded by Omani security personnel, some in jeeps and some on foot. At the front door three plain-clothed guards check the guests.

Such precautions were necessary considering the political situation in the region. A few months earlier (March 2003), the United States started the invasion of Iraq. The response in the Middle East countries was unknown at the time.

There were about one hundred guests—mostly Omanis. A few Embassy employees were present. The Embassy employee in charge of the Fulbright program announced the name of each of the two scholars. Every one was then invited to enjoy the dinner.

The night of this reception had an indelible mark in our memory. The honor bestowed on us is something we will cherish forever.

Because of the volatility of the regional political situation, the American Embassy kept us on the alert list to be notified in case of an emergency that may require certain actions. This in itself made us feel safe.

CHAPTER 17

OUR MISSION?

The author dedicates this chapter to be an overview of our three daughters' lives albeit being mentioned on and off in previous chapters. Instead of using the first person, the author opts to use "we" (my wife and I) as a result of a conviction that raising a child is a two-person responsibility. It is enough of an arduous job to be handled by both a father and a mother that my heart goes out for single parents who, for various reasons, had to go through it alone. The father provides discipline (beside other contributions) and the mother provides love and care (again on top of many other needs).

Both discipline and love, not necessarily in this order, seem to be essential ingredients for the future well-being of a youngster.

As parents in the autumn of our lives we sometimes ask ourselves: what is our mission in life? Just to eat, drink, work, spend time with family and friends then die? Nothing is wrong with any of the above, it is actually the normal life of normal people.

But is there a higher purpose for life (second to worshiping God)?

The Lord said that children are a gift from Him. No wonder, then, to notice the deep intrinsic desire for all humans to marry and form a family. This holds true even in the 21st century with new "lifestyles" emerging. Interestingly enough, those who attack the institution of marriage as irrelevant still seek and fight for their right to adopt children—children who have been brought to life by a male and a female (married or not is a moral problem, not a structural one).

The question of our mission as parents becomes more relevant as we approach this stage of life when things quiet down considerably: no more worries about a career, and the children are all grown ups and settled in their own homes and families.

It was our feelings of responsibility toward our daughters and their future that, directly or indirectly, contributed to our decision to leaving our extended families in Egypt and move to the United States.

It is the author's conviction that parents (not schools nor the government) have the responsibility of providing the best possible opportunities for the children to grow up as good, productive members of society.

Even in the early 1980s, when we moved to the U. S., Egypt's future seemed uncertain at best, and predictably bleak. Over the past 30 years, these predictions proved correct.

Thank God we had the initiative to make the not-so-easy decision of moving to America when my wife and I were in our 40s, and our daughters ranged in age from seven months to 10 years.

Was it an easy transition? Not so.

In subsequent years in the U. S. we encountered the "dating" conundrum.

Some American parents face the same problem. What makes the situation more crucial for people moving from most Middle Eastern cultures is that the latter tend to limit intermingling between the two sexes. However, having more females pursuing their education through college and beyond had rendered such a separation moot. But still Egyptian society was not at ease with girls going out with boys.

To illustrate, in Egypt, girls attended public schools (grade, middle and high) that are only for girls. However, most private schools, especially those that stress foreign languages, have mixed classes.

In college, however, both sexes attend the same classes. But intermingling stops there. It is not the norm that a male student goes out with a female student, or goes to her house to study together.

"Dating" as understood in Western culture is practically nonexistent in Egypt.

In marriage, the bride is to be a virgin. If a girl is found pregnant before getting married, the family faces a disaster. The matter does not only bring great embarrassment, but all family members would be ostracized from society. Years back, in Upper Egypt, such an action could lead to the girl being killed by one of her family members (honor killing).

It may not be hard, then, to understand the reaction to such an impertinent act (pregnancy out of wedlock) if one considers the social environment of a country like Egypt. Extended families tend to live nearby. What other family members do or say concerns and affects all family members. Any wrongdoing would be the subject of conversation for quite some time and may never be forgotten.

Disrepute seems to withstand time.

Such is the nature of the culture we lived in for so many years before moving to our new society where "dating" is the norm.

Dawlat and I had to face the dilemma—one way or the other. We understood peer pressure, and how crucial for teenagers to blend in, and to avoid the appearance of otherwise being odd.

A delicate balance had to be struck. Allowing dating, we felt, should be coupled with open and free discussions at home—at the kitchen table.

As all parents experience, teenagers consider themselves the more intelligent, knowledgeable and in touch with the times. They believe that endows them with better judgment whenever a controversy arises about their lives. We spent some time figuring out the conundrum.

Shall we, the parents, say: "because we said so," or simply let them do what the others do and hope for the best?

The first of the two options would only lead to rebellion. Many a family tried enforcing their points of view and ended up regretting such an approach as the daughter left the security of home.

Choosing to simply avoid the conversation and allow for peer pressure and the entertainment industry to be the guiding beacon could have some adverse, if not disastrous, consequences.

A case in point. In the early 1980s, watching TV programs was for all the family to enjoy; no profanity or sexual content. By the 2000s, however, hardly any program was devoid of violence, profanity, sex or all of the above.

It gradually dawned on us that if we sought an impact on our daughters' view of morality we needed to invoke some sort of a higher authority.

The Word of God, it seemed, could deal with the dissonance. During discussions we would say: OK, let us see what God says. Their argument usually faded henceforth.

A believer or not, God's Word protects us from others as well as from ourselves. It is not intended to rob us from world pleasures but guide us to the proper way of enjoying His blessings.

Almost every night we, as a family, had dinner together. Sometimes, without planning, the conversation carries us in a direction that invites edifying. Rather than quoting verse and chapter, we opted to talk about our actual life experiences.

Describing how Divine interventions guided our path both before and after moving to the United States might be more effective in guiding them to the right direction.

Could it be that the human mind can relate directly to real-world occurrences as opposed to mere quotations—even from the Bible? If what actually took place in life could address the mind to establish the foundation for a belief in a higher authority (Divine intervention), then quoting the Word of God could reach both the heart and the mind.

At this critical period in the life of young men and women, they are bombarded with limitless numbers of temptations. Even home schooling protects only so far, and for a limited period. Eventually, our sons and daughters would be immersed in the society. If we, as parents, could deal with their inquiring minds to provide some reasoning that helps them to winnow good from evil, then it would be easier to endear God to their hearts.

If the mind responds positively, hopefully the heart would follow.

There might be different approaches to convince our children that the human being has been created for a reason by an Intelligent

Designer—another term to describe God. The age of the addressee(s) may help decide among the available approaches.

In our case, our two elder daughters were in their teen-age years (the third was still a young girl). We chose to talk about incidents that we did not have much control over.

To reiterate the incident in chapter 5, the author described how it felt to drive a fast-moving car on an oil-covered, slippery, winding two-lane country road on a hot summer day. With no control whatsoever on the vehicle, an oncoming fast-moving bus put me face to face with death.

But, the guardian angel kept me safe.

On another occasion the author talked about how a young gentleman, named Milad, at the airline counter at Cairo airport held the "keys" to our new life in the United States (chapter 6).

Milad, a Christian, sympathized with a Christian family that was on its way to a new life in America. It was not hard for us to know that Milad was a Christian since Muslims never use the name; by the same token, Milad knew that we are Christians since the name Bishara is exclusively used by Christians. (Egyptian passports list the religion).

Did we ever have any control over choosing Milad (or another Christian) to handle our papers at the airport?!

Or how the "circumstances" enabled the author to join the State of Kansas civil service, back in 1983, against the will of a high-ranking official? (chapter 11).

Many years later, in 1999, the same individual who selected the author for the first job with the State of Kansas provided valuable advice that enabled me to claim the patent against the will of yet another high-ranking official (chapter 16).

How could all this have happened just by chance? At least to the author, it seemed highly improbable.

A more likely interpretation is a Divine intervention.

My wife, Dawlat, talked about her work experience here in the United States (chapter 12).

How she put aside her Ph. D. degree to work in a nursery (she loved the little ones).

Her first job in the State of Kansas civil service was a pharmacy technician that requires the equivalent of a high-school diploma. Then her persistence and effort paid off when a vacancy for a programmer analyst (II) became available. Her chances of getting such a job were slim or actually nonexistent. But, through a set of "circumstances" that preexisted in the organization, Dawlat was offered the job!

The supervisor that selected Dawlat for the job was first excluded from the selection committee. The supervisor strongly objected and the situation corrected—as she told Dawlat later on.

Dawlat continued with the same agency till she retired in 2003, and in the meantime got two promotions first to programmer analyst III then IV.

We always wondered if the particular supervisor who chose Dawlat was never brought on the selection committee would Dawlat have been offered the position?

It is hard to tell. It is true that she had got a Ph. D. in physics and 21 semester credit hours in computer programming but, at the time, had no hands-on programming experience. If another applicant had no college degree but hands-on experience would s/he have been preferred? (In the 1980s, many programming jobs went to experienced employees with no degrees). It is true that Dawlat's future performance on the job proved her capability, but how could the interviewing committee foretell?

We cited these actual-life occurrences to convince our daughters (or others for that matter) that there is an unseen power that controls our lives. Obviously, some people might exclude the idea out-of-hand as irrelevant. That is a decision for everyone to make.

An important aspect that we sought to instill in our children is respect of the elders. This includes not only the parents and grandparents but generally those who have been longer in life and have experienced its vicissitudes.

If we listen carefully there is usually something to learn from others. But we would not listen if we are under the impression that we know it all—the natural tendency of teenagers.

As parents, we encouraged our daughters to reprogram their minds to be open to lessons worthy of remembering. As energy is synonymous with youth, wisdom comes with age—usually.

While in her junior year in high school, Heba, our eldest daughter, decided to audit for the high school orchestra. She already had some home lessons in violin and flute but never shared in extra-curricular activities at school. This was her first trial.

The music teacher was taken by surprise to see a new face auditing for the first time while in her junior year. Students do this usually in their first year in high school.

Heba got a spot in the high-school orchestra.

Heba joined Kansas State University (KSU) in the Fall of 1988—she was 17 years old. At the time, Dawlat had just got her new job as a programmer, and the author had only been for one year in the new capacity as a research chemist—both of us working for the State of Kansas. Kansas civil service provided good benefits and job security as opposed to the private sector with its higher salaries but not much security. For the sake of our daughters and the continuity of their education, the state jobs were a blessing.

But higher education is not cheap—even in the late 1980s, and more so now. It was not an option but a priority. This meant that we needed to be wise with our resources.

Being unaccustomed to credit (at the time, Egypt had no credit cards) put more self-restraints on our spending. The ultimate goal, however, was well worthwhile.

Dawlat and I kept our daughters abreast of our financial situation. They were appreciative—most of the time.

It was not hard for them to realize that we did not waste money on any item, and this probably made the situation easy to live with. The positive outcome, though, was for them to find out that life does not always provide all what we want. The desires are endless, and unless we manage to put a cap on them we will just be miserable.

Once in college, Heba started getting applications for credit cards (now students get applications when in high school). It did not seem fair to subject a 17-year old to the allure of buying stuff on credit. Parental guidance was in demand.

Dawlat and I made it clear that credit cards can be used to the extent that one plans to pay the balance in full when due.

As many parents did, we paid tuition, room and board, books and pocket money. In the sophomore year, Heba pledged a sorority and lived in one of KSU sororities.

In the Spring of 1993 (at the age of 22) she graduated with a degree in chemical engineering (GPA 3.3).

After working for one year as a chemist, she applied and was admitted to the Medical school of the University of Oklahoma, Oklahoma City. After graduation in 1998, she had her residency with the University of Kansas (KU) Medical school—Wichita campus. Since 2001 Heba has been a practicing physician (family medicine) in Wichita, Kansas.

In July 2001 she got married to a KSU graduate who had got a degree in civil engineering—he is working as a consulting engineer in Wichita, Kansas.

Although both of them were students at the same college, they never met. It was years later when each of them, separately, attended Central Christian church in Wichita. In a Bible study class they realized that they were both KSU engineering graduates. If you, the reader, have got the chance to know a KSU graduate, then you realize how gleeful it was for the two of them to meet.

Heba and Paul live in Wichita, Kansas and have Samuel and Hannah.

Rasha, our middle daughter, had a different encounter.

In high school, Rasha audited for and got a spot on the sheer leading team. She was a cheerleader for most of her high school years. She was also a cheerleader in her first year at Kansas State University.

In the summer preceding her senior year in high school, she worked part-time at Vista fast-food restaurant. There, she met Tom. He also worked there part-time.

After her senior year, Rasha attended the college of engineering, KSU in Manhattan, Kansas, starting in the Fall of 1990; she was 17-years old. The following year, Tom got his high school diploma and also attended KSU engineering. He chose industrial engineering while Rasha got into chemical engineering.

Needless to say they saw each other regularly.

Rasha graduated in the Spring of 1996 (at the age of 23 and a GPA of 3.0). She got an interview with Kansas Department of Health and Environment (KDHE) a couple of weeks before she actually graduated. She was offered the job, and in June 1996 she started working at KDHE, Air Pollution section, in Topeka, Kansas. Tom continued his studies at KSU in Manhattan, Kansas.

In May 1997, Tom and Rasha got married, and in 1999 bought their first house in Topeka. Tom chose to commute every day to Manhattan—more than one-hour drive each way. He is now working at KDOT, Right of Way.

A few years later (2009) Rasha and Tom moved to a better and larger house in a neighborhood with good schools. Their first-born, Gabriel, is doing well in grade school and sports.

Some health issues prevented their having more children. Adoption was an alternative. Through a local church (Topeka Bible Church) the process of adoption proceeded slowly but with no surprises. In January 2010, Noah arrived with Rasha, Tom and Gabriel to the United States. Born in Taiwan, Noah was two years old at the time.

Our youngest daughter, Shahira, proved to have a different mind set when it came to future college studies.

Since Shahira was four-years old she got involved first in ballet, then as she grew in years got in modern and tap dancing as well. She played every year in the Nutcracker performance. Shahira continued this activity until she graduated from high school. In high school she was a cheerleader.

Whereas her two older sisters followed the parents' suit and pursued science-and mathematics-based curricula, she opted for humanities and social studies.

After attending the University of Kansas (KU), Lawrence, Shahira got a B. S. degree from the School of Journalism. She graduated in the spring of 2003 at the age of 22 and a GPA of 2.8.

In June 2003 Shahira and Eric got married. The two of them had attended the same high school but it was only in their senior year that they started their love relationship. Following high school, Eric attended KSU in Manhattan while Shahira went to KU in Lawrence. The 90-mile distance between the two did not trammel their ability to see each other. Topeka, about half the distance from each, provided a reasonable location especially that the two sets of parents were Topekans.

That Shahira selected this line of study (Journalism) proved to be a blessing. It simply fit her natural, God-given talents.

Since her infant years, Shahira was a sociable person who easily made friends. Her ability to argue confounded the author on numerous occasions. A case in point: In her high-school years when she asked for an item that we thought to be a bit excessive, our answer was that her older sisters could do without it. She would respond: "Is this my fault?"

To be fair, though, our finances at the time were on the rise; Heba had graduated from her undergraduate studies, the same as Rasha who had graduated and was working. The decrease in our obligations was coupled with the normal, gradual increase in income. Shahira, usually, got what she wanted.

Did this extra care breed any unintended consequences? Not at all. At the age of 26 Shahira worked as the Director of Marketing and Communication for four Kansas associations. She is highly conscientious about her family (Shahira and Eric now have two-year old twins: a boy, Cole, and a girl, Avry), and about her job.

Eric, Shahira's husband, is now working as Senior Director of Government Affairs, Kansas Chamber of Commerce.

The author tends to believe that love and care would not spoil a child. A mixture of love, involvement, concern, sacrifice and, yes, discipline when called for, are necessary ingredients for the healthy development of our children. Over all the years of their studies from grade school to college, Dawlat and I were there—looking at grade reports, exams and quizzes. Though sometimes felt goaded, our daughters knew that it was out of love and concern about their future. As they got older they became even more appreciative of our involvement.

Talking about raising children was the subject of an interesting article in TIME, January 31, 2011, p. 34, by Annie Murphy Paul. The article discusses a book by Amy Chua, Yale Law professor, entitled: "Battle Hymn of the Tiger Mother," that describes how Chua raised her two daughters.

Paul wrote:

> "Her stories of never accepting a grade lower than an A, of insisting on hours of math and spelling drills and piano and violin practice each day, of not allowing playdates or sleepovers or television or computer games or even school plays, ... have left many readers outraged but also defensive . . . . Westerners often laud their children as "talented" or "gifted," Chua says, while Asian parents highlight the importance of hard work . . . . Chua goes on to say: . . . . nothing is fun until you are good at it. Now, Chua says: she was perhaps too severe in enforcing long hours of practice . . . . but kids really shouldn't be able to take the easy way out."

Paul commented: "The tiger-mother approach isn't an ethnicity but a philosophy; expect the best from your children, and don't settle for anything less."

Hara E.Marano, editor-at-large of Psychology Today magazine, says: " . . . . American parenting, at its best, combines ambitious expectations and a loving environment with a respect for each child's individual differences . . . . "

Paul's article concluded by saying Chua's tale is "the tale of an immigrant striver, determined to make a better life for himself and his family in a nation where such dreams are still possible . . . . Hard work, persistence, no patience for excuses . . . . sounds like a prescription for success."

Luckily, Dawlat and I had followed the prescription before we read about it—in 2011.

Heba and Rasha proceeded through their education without much interference on our side. Never had to push for doing home work or study more hours at home. They knew their responsibilities and took it seriously.

Was it helpful for our daughters to see us, the parents, bring our work home? Dawlat spent long hours at home studying for computer classes while she worked full-time (from 8:00 to 5:00) The author, especially starting in 1987, brought home research data and research articles to work on.

Was this environment conducive to the learning process of our daughters?

It is true that we did not push for study but our interest and concern were not in doubt. Our keen interest expressed itself as we asked for test results, grades, ...

At home, we had dinner together—almost every night. The kitchen table was a prime location for communication within family members.

Without planning, the conversation sometimes presented an opportunity to talk about some life experience that is worth remembering as it draws on some type of wisdom.

For our youngest, Shahira, the circumstances dictated another approach.

Her grade school was a private, church-affiliated one that used the "pace" method of learning. The "pace" system left it open for a student to proceed at his/her own speed. Once the student finishes a "pace," it got graded and another "pace" with a higher serial number is started.

Dawlat pushed Shahira in all subjects (Chua's approach). Within a year or two, Shahira was at the top of her class—compared to her class mates, she worked on the "paces" with the highest serial numbers in mathematics, science and reading.

The impact of such a pressure did not show up except years later—in college.

Shahira apparently lost interest in science and mathematics altogether. Her freshman year in college was geared toward a science major as a step toward, probably, medical school. She passed all courses, but the grades were mostly Bs and Cs. The grades for social studies and humanities faired much better than science and mathematics.

It took a lot of conversation and thinking to settle down on a major for her college degree. The University of Kansas had a top-class school of Journalism. As it proved later, the choice was the best for Shahira. Since her youth, she was sociable, easy to make friends, communicate, and debate.

The God-given talents fit her studies and career quite well.

Dawlat and I did not see eye to eye on every issue but thank God we had similar ideas about raising our daughters. Were we perfect parents? Certainly not. Did we make mistakes? For sure. But we did our best.

If our daughters came out fine it was simply God's blessing—our greatest blessing.

The Lord has blessed us with three wonderful sons-in-law: Paul, Tom and Eric. It is hard to say who is better than the other.

After Shahira got married in June 2003, Dawlat retired and we both flew to Muscat, Oman to start the author's Fulbright scholarship (chapter 16). A few years later, the author retired, and in September 2006, Dawlat and I moved to our new condominium in Florida where we live now.

The setting of our new property can hardly be surpassed. From our balcony we have a panoramic view of the clear blue water of the Gulf of Mexico as it touches the white sands on the beach.

The only drawback is the one-thousand miles that separate us from our children and grandchildren.

Our great joy comes when we drive to Kansas to spend time with our "big" family. We have three homes with six grandchildren (we recently leased a property in Topeka to live in while visiting in Kansas).

It is at this stage of our lives when we realize that life had offered what it had—our hopes become trammeled by what we had already got. This is our lot; it is too late to make much of a change. Time to reap what one had sown.

No wonder the Word of God says that children are a gift from Him upon whom we, the parents, are to be held accountable.

PART IV

BETWEEN TWO CULTURES: MIDDLE EASTERN AND WESTERN

CHAPTER 18

A NEWCOMER TO A DIFFERENT CULTURE

The West is clearly defined as Europe and the United States. The East, on the other hand, is less clearly defined. For example, does Japan conform to the East? Does Russia?

For the sake of the present argument, however, we will consider Egypt as an Eastern culture which by any measure does not stretch the actual facts.

The word culture is widely used to describe various aspects of life though sometimes the exact meaning of the word seems blurred. It may be worthwhile, then, to find out what the word "culture" really entails.

The American Heritage Dictionary of the English language (William Morris, Editor. Boston: Houghton Mifflin, 1978), defines culture as: "the totality of socially transmitted behavior patterns, arts, beliefs, institutions, and all other products of human work and thought characteristic of a community or population."

Dealing with cultural issues carries its own risks. After all, culture covers the integration of a wide variety of physical and mental activities that defines a group of people.

Two parameters immediately impose themselves: time and location.

1-Time: Cultural attributes are subject to change over time. In the second half of the 19th century the Industrial revolution in America had its footprints—family members moved away seeking jobs in manufacturing in the Northeast. Big cities grew even bigger.

The industrialization of the West Coast and the Atlantic coast states is a fairly recent phenomenon. The Midwestern states East of the Missouri river, the so-called "rust belt," were industrialized after the Civil War, although they retained much of their rural character. For example, the industrial output of Iowa usually exceeds in value its agricultural output.

Fast forward to the second half of the 20th century when the electronic "revolution" came into play.

From TV, with 24-hour news channels, to the computer and the Internet, then to "smart" phones. The electronic innovations affected Eastern and Western cultures as well, though to different degrees.

2-Location: Even within one and the same country, the geographic location can not be overlooked as a contributor to cultural change.

Southwestern states such as California, New Mexico, Arizona and Texas have seen an influx of Hispanic population that added another dimension to the cultural heritage.

A parallel phenomenon occurred in Egypt though on a different time scale. Upper (southern) Egypt had a considerable number of Sudanese people who moved north at times when Egypt was a prosperous country that offered better opportunities. Northern Egypt, however, had been exposed to quite a number of foreign cultures from Asia as well as from Europe. Overlooking the Mediterranean Sea, and at the junction between Africa and Asia, Egypt's strategic location has been a double-aged sword. Since decline of the Ancient Egyptian civilization, around 500 B. C., successive invaders occupied Egypt for the most part of its history.

So, talking about the current Egyptian culture, or any other culture for that matter, one must consider the "totality of socially transmitted behavior patterns, ... ," as defined by the American Heritage Dictionary.

Understanding a culture is hardly achieved by reading a book, watching a TV program, taking a course, or even learning its language. Because it is intangible, culture can easily be illusive and misconstrued.

In his book "The Fourth World War," Alexandre de Marenches, former Director of French Intelligence, (William Morrow and Company, 1992, p.21) wrote:

> "I have learned that there are two sorts of history. There is history that we see and hear, the official history; and there is the secret history—the things that happen behind the scenes, in the dark, that go bump in the night. When one has a true world view, both become comprehensible. Both are essential."

The term "culture" might replace "history" in the above quote.

The author encountered many unfamiliar facets of American culture in the earliest years of living in his new home country. Prior familiarity with the English language was no substitute for the effort expended in comprehending the American society.

In Egypt, the English language is compulsory: two years in grade school, two years in junior high, and three years in high school. In college, all courses in science, mathematics, and engineering are taught in English. But knowing the language is but the first step in daily-life communication.

The author was born and lived for 40 years in an Eastern culture before moving to the United States 30 years ago.

When it comes to culture, knowing about a culture and living in it are two different aspects—the first is no substitute for the second.

With enough time and distance, it seemed interesting to look back at the Egyptian culture (as representative of a region) in the light of the American culture (as representative of the West).

To be sure, significant and crucial differences do exist—as might conceivably be expected.

Some cultural dimensions may not be so crucial to the underlying development of a nation. So long as a given society agrees on a certain way of doing something, then this would be the norm for that society. For example, in Egypt lunch is served at two or three in the afternoon and it is the main meal. In the U. S. dinner, at about six o'clock in the evening is the main meal.

But several other cultural criteria have a fundamental role in advancing or pulling a society backwards. Is there a price a society has to pay in order to achieve success and prosperity? Should a culture remain unchanged regardless of past failure? The answer to such open questions may call for some elaboration.

In the United States, and because of job opportunities for the author and for my wife, we have been living in rather small-to medium-sized cities with no Egyptian-Americans to socialize with. This, though hard at the beginning, proved to be a blessing.

We were suddenly catapulted 100 percent into the American society. The author have seen other Egyptian-American families in big cities such as Houston, Texas and Kansas City, Kansas who socialize in the most part, if not totally, with others of the same culture. For Christians, the Coptic Orthodox church of Egypt responded to the needs of Egyptian-Americans living in the big cities by opening a number of churches—about 50 in the 1990s. Such places of worship allured Christian immigrants from Egypt, and provided a social environment not much different from that back home. In a sense, this could have inhibited the ability to understand and mix with the American culture. The same principle applies for Muslim immigrants.

It is quite remarkable, though, that, on the whole, the American society does a great job of assimilating the newcomers. Quite the contrast with Europe. But, moving from one culture to another will never be easy.

On p.22 of the March 10, 2008 issue of NEWSWEEK, Robert Kosi Tette talks about his emigration from Ghana to the U. S., and about his struggle in his new country:

> "Every inch of progress, however, had been achieved through exhausting battles . . . . adjusting to corporate culture exacted another toll. Initially I found myself putting in twice the effort just to keep up. I learned to feign assertiveness after realizing that I would not be taken seriously otherwise . . . . Enlightenment had come with the loss of innocence and a silent struggle. My

> cultural dichotomy was no different from what other immigrants from other cultures faced in America. I could stop dwelling on being torn between two countries by accepting my new identity as a progressive blend of the two."

The author tends to believe that the struggle of Mr. Tette would decrease with the passage of time (he wrote his article 10 years from his arrival in the U. S.). As the roots get deeper into the ground the blurring goes away and identity crystallization becomes unquestionable.

Firoozeh Dumas and Gus Lee, (Jennifer Traig, Editor. Autobiographer Handbook, New York: Henry Holt and Company, 2008), both long-time immigrants to the U. S., describe their feelings of responsibility to reveal their respective cultures to the American society.

Dumas says: "Ever since I was seven, I have basically been an unpaid ambassador. To some degree, this happens to all immigrants . . . . I always wanted to make Americans understand Iran and vice versa."

Lee, from Shanghai, states that: "A different culture is scary when viewed through narrowed eyes and with a racing pulse; that same culture, viewed with a brave friend and an open heart, it becomes the world."

Following 9/11, American interest in the Middle-Eastern culture grew exponentially.

Even though the region as a whole shares many common aspects, it is logical to observe a number of differences. History, exposure to the outside world and proximity to other cultures are but some contributing factors.

The Lebanese and Syrians (on the Mediterranean Sea) like to do business and trade; Egyptians (the Ancient Egyptians excelled in architecture, medicine and astronomy) like to have as many degrees as they could possibly get; and the Iraqis tend to be more violent than the others.

In the following few chapters the emphasis will be on the Egyptian culture in particular, in an attempt to make the Americans more aware of its intricacies. Where appropriate, a reference to the American culture will be made.

The topics listed below were not arranged according to significance.

CHAPTER 19

SOCIOECONOMIC FACTORS

Egypt has limited natural resources. Crude oil barely covers domestic consumption. There has been a lot of talk about exploring new wells especially in the Western Desert, but nothing had materialized, yet. It is interesting to note that Libya, on the western border of Egypt, is a major oil-exporting country (1.8 million barrels a day) whereas the Egyptian Western Desert that borders Libya has almost nil. Sudan, south of Egypt, has plenty of oil, same as Saudi Arabia to the east (9 million barrels a day). Are there reasons for the discrepancy?

Egypt's population has been increasing uncontrolled. With a population of over 80 million, and an agricultural land area that remained practically the same over the centuries, it stands to reason that the economy suffered.

Add to the equation four wars that involved Israel: 1948, 1956, 1967 and 1973. In the early 1960s, Egypt sent armies to Yemen. At the time Egypt was united with Syria and trials were underway to include Yemen in the coalition. The war in Yemen, as well as the other four wars, proved very costly to the Egyptian economy—and the Egyptian people.

Putting wars aside, the 1960s have seen the continuation of a trend that started in 1956 with the nationalization of the Suez Canal Authority. Socialism spread as a fire in a dry forest (see also chapter 2).

The regime that existed prior to the 1952 revolution was persistently depicted as a corrupt, capitalist system that deprived most people of wealth to the benefit of a few. All private corporations, banks, and businesses were nationalized; homes, cars and all personal possessions of the wealthy were taken away. This pleased the masses. All decisions were entirely political.

To gain further popularity, big farms were divided into small parcels and given to farmers who could hardly afford caring for the newly-acquired land, let alone paying the rent to the once-rich "owners." The original owner lost control over his property; his only "right" was to collect the rent from the farmer who was chosen by the government to cultivate the land. More often than not, the farmer evaded attempts by the owner to collect the rent. The system sided with the farmer, and he knew it.

Housing took a parallel, disastrous hit. Big cities in Egypt used to have a limited number of single-family homes, called "villas." The majority of housing was available as high rise buildings with multiple units for rent. It used to be that the landlord decided the monthly rent—based on the market's supply and demand.

In the early 1960s the government stepped in. The rent was to be decided based on a decision made by a city/county commission that visits each new building, makes its calculations and determines the rent. Obviously these commissions were aware of the new official trend underlying the whole process—that is, to keep the rent as low as possible.

Landlords of buildings existing before the new law were ordered to maintain the rent frozen at the early 1960s value; this is true even as of now—five decades later, and with sky-rocketing inflation. Tenants of some nice apartments in nice neighborhoods that were built before and during the 1960s and the 1970s now pay a monthly rent that is equivalent to a kilo (2.22 pounds) of fruit!

The 1960s have also seen Egypt being catapulted into industry. The intentions were good but executing wrong policies proved harmful to the economy. Abrupt, hastily adopted changes such as these never work—whether in Egypt or elsewhere. Culture takes a long time to adapt.

The last two or three decades, however, have seen several correcting steps to reverse this slippery trend and to take the country away from such ill-conceived policies. But considerable damage had occurred; some consequences may be irreversible.

The adoption of some degree of socialism had created a sense of non-ownership or detachment.

Nationalized institutions belonged to no one—they belonged to every one!

The absence of legitimate entities to channel protests, complaints and the report of wrongdoings led to a state of lawlessness and even chaos. Those with connections became the powerful. No matter what the qualifications or experience someone might have, so long as you know someone up there you will be fine. Favoritism dominated the society. With no free press, or media in general, rumors abounded. To be sure, some rumors were exaggerated, some were flat wrong and many were true. And there lay the danger. The general public was deprived the means to know what was going on.

To illustrate. A well-connected, high-ranking official took a bribe. A rumor started. It could not be political—no political parties were allowed at the time. The media outlets were silent. The rumor was left to fester. The Egyptian society enjoys talking about every aspect of politics especially when it comes to a scandal (a human impulse in all societies). Politics, and every trivia associated with it, is a favorite subject of conversation. In Egypt, politics is not a taboo, and everyone is expected to have an opinion—about every issue.

What would be the residual effect of such a rumor? What is the cumulative effect?

Does such an environment lead to a feeling of not belonging, chagrin and helplessness? It certainly did.

Immediately before the 1967 war, the Egyptian army was nicely spread in the flat Sinai Peninsula without much protection from air strikes. When Israel started its preemptive attack, the state of chaos that engulfed the armed forces was not unexpected.

To defend a regime—to sacrifice your life in war, there should be a conscious belief that you are defending a fair and just system. Deep inside, almost everyone knew that fairness and justice were non-existent.

The fact that the defeat in 1967 was psychological and not professional is seen in the light of the 1973 war.

Over a six-year period a change in the Egyptian leadership, not the rank and file, brought a dramatic change in performance of the Egyptian armed forces.

In 1973 the Egyptian army succeeded in crossing the Suez Canal, on the East side of which the Israeli army had already built the "impenetrable" Bar-Lev line of defense that was supposed to prevent such an attack. As the war progressed in favor of Egypt, and Israel became in immediate danger, the United States stepped in.

Separating the 1967 and 1973 wars was a transition in political leadership. The latter war proved a moral booster that came after a number of unsuccessful military conflicts involving Egypt.

On top of that, there was a reversal in the economic policy that brought glee to the intelligentsia. Socialism was abolished. Over time, all nationalized institutions were converted into private entities.

Allegiance to the Soviet Union was terminated. Economically, Egypt was back on the right track.

But culturally, the scars of the 1960s proved harder to cure. The animosity between the haves and have-nots kept growing. Hard economic times kept eating at the already limited pie. And as the pie got smaller resentment flourished. Distrust became the norm; distrust between the citizens and the government as well as distrust between the people themselves.

As trivial as it may sound, the lack of social trust is detrimental to progress. Human energy and time are dissipated in designing defense mechanisms to combat those who are presumed dishonest. The latter become more adept in circumventing the new rules. Newer and more strict regulations have to be put in place. And so on.

In such an environment, bribes abound as bureaucrats abuse their authority in the maze of rules and regulations. This only feeds the chagrin of citizenry.

Recently, banks in Egypt started a credit-card system. But with a twist. The credit-card holder must make a cash deposit, the amount of which limits his/her credit line.

Tied up to the prevailing atmosphere of distrust among Egyptians is the assumption of guilt. Perfectly logical. If there is no trust then every body is guilty—until, somehow, proven otherwise!

Talk about progress trammeled by unseen forces.

The author can not keep himself from pondering the underlying societal belief in the U. S. that everyone is innocent until proven otherwise. The burden of proof is on the authorities to prove, beyond reasonable doubt, that a citizen is guilty.

From where did this assumption of innocence emerge? Is it not the Declaration of Independence that asserts that all men are endowed by their Creator with certain unalienable rights? Freedom stands as the cornerstone upon which the social fabric is built. Freedom of speech, freedom of worship, freedom to vote, think, and even carry arms. The system assumes that all are responsible citizens who behave accordingly. It works because this is actually the case—the majority are law-abiding people. The system can not, and should not, be held hostage for the misbehavior of a few.

But this leads to another question.

Why does the majority in one country obey the law whereas the opposite prevails in another society?

A number of factors spring to mind. The collective wealth; a fair judicial system; free media outlets; a healthy political environment (democratic institutions); and, undoubtedly, religion.

With the exception of religion, all of the above factors are interrelated and interdependent. The media (the Fourth Estate) is essential in maintaining functioning democratic entities, and a good judicial system guarantees no malice through exposing some incidents. The American Constitution has safeguards against usurpation of power by any of the three branches: legislative, judicial or executive. In such an environment most members of society develop a conscious feeling of stability. Most people obey the law regardless of who or how wealthy they are—most of the time.

So where does religion fits in? The author likes to suggest that religion is the foundation of culture.

Since the beginning of creation, the human being sought "something" to worship. As if it is a built-in mechanism where man (in the generic sense) felt that there must be a higher authority larger than him. Early on he built idols. Then he worshiped the Sun—the source of light and heat. Then worship moved from the tangible to the intangible. This was a big leap. It defied how the human being relates to the outside world. We believe in our senses. I see a building, I am sure it exists; I hear a plane flying above that I can also see, then this is a plane.

But to believe in the unseen, this is faith.

Because of the imperative role religion plays in a culture, the author would like to designate a separate chapter for religion.

CHAPTER 20

RELIGION

The Founding Fathers, when they wrote the Constitution, thought of the indelible effects of the atrocities associated with the Church over a period when it controlled the political arena.

At the time of the adoption of the First Amendment to the U. S. Constitution, several of the states had state churches. In some of the Northern states, the Congregational church was the state church and all citizens paid a tax to support it. In Virginia, the state church was the Episcopal church. In the early 1800s, these states rescinded official recognition of specific denominations. The First Amendment applied only to the Federal government until the adoption of the 14th Amendment after the Civil War.

The separation between Church and State has been in effect ever since.

But on the individual scale, every human being—consciously or subconsciously, has a set of beliefs, or a world view, that shapes his or her behavior and relationships. This holds true for atheism.

It therefore remains that human behavior is, to a great extent, the product of some sort of belief system. The doctrine of separation between Church and State intended to limit the political influence of Church as an institution, but did not seek to eradicate Christianity from the daily lives of the citizenry. It is actually impossible to remove religion from the heart and mind of people—even if a political system tried. For 70 years the Communists in the then Soviet Union could not prevent some elderly people from reading their Bible. And eventually, that political system collapsed.

The author was happily astonished, in the inchoate years in the U. S., to hear preachers pray for the government to succeed.

Even recently, with a liberal Democratic administration, there is that sense of deep Christian teachings that can not be mistaken.

Jon Meacham, former NEWSWEEK editor and Pulitzer prize winner, in an article entitled: "Realism we can believe in," NEWSWEEK, December 4, 2008, p.8, put it this way:

> "Here, then, is Obama's vision of America as a city upon a hill: we are an exceptional nation but ours is an exceptionalism that imposes as many burdens as it does blessings . . . . it is an exceptionalism of obligation—to whom much is given, much is expected."

The thought lies right at the heart of Christianity.

Others, like Walter Williams, Northwest Florida Daily News, October 23, 2009, attribute the American exceptionalism to the "deep distrust and suspicion" of the government. Well, the Founders, more than 200 years ago, put safeguards—of checks and balances—against human impulse of control. This worked well and bred a political system that is a model and envy of much of the world. To claim that "distrust and suspicion" control the American society is hard to accept—at least to the author. It may be true that over the history of the U. S. some incidents raised questions about the possible role of government and how it responded or caused certain outcomes. But again, humans are not angels nor perfect.

Consider the following. The popularity of social networking, for example Facebook has 600 million subscribers worldwide including nearly one hundred fifty million Americans, is a sign of trust that propels individuals to share personal information with "friends."

It may well be that the "deep distrust and suspicion" of the government is not as much of a structural phenomenon as it is just a political strategy.

In the November 15, 2010 issue of TIME, p. 44, Richard Norton Smith, in his article: "Hoping for Audacity. How John F. Kennedy grew into the presidency, and what it means for Obama," wrote: " .... Ronald Reagen declared government more problem than problem solver. By 2009, confidence in Washington had been dulled by [two] decades of deception, media scorn and a popular questioning of authority at all levels."

Here it is. Distrust in the government is a political platform for one of the two political parties with the belief that government should be small, and allow people to do business without much interference. The events of the 2008 Great Recession, however, proved otherwise. But this is beside the point.

The fact remains that political policies are both debatable and reversible—they rarely interfere with the mutual trust between the citizenry in their daily life. This is in contrast to other societies where distrust is deeply rooted in some religious beliefs that extend back for almost a millennium and a half, and transcend all aspects of social and economic life (discussed in more detail later in this chapter).

Over 30 years, the author has lived in the U. S. and found that trust dominates the land. This is true on the individual level as well as in the way the government treats the citizenry. This may not be surprising since Christianity offers a way of living. At its heart, Christianity is pure and ideal. It may be true that the human being is not perfect nor ideal, but we have our Lord to look at and try to live our lives as He did.

The author tends to think that prosperity of the West in general and the United States in particular is attributable, in the most part, to Christianity and its principles. A culture that believes in, and practices, love, forgiveness, trust, and caring for the needy does provide a social environment that is conducive to honesty, harmony and hard work.

It may be true that over the last two or three decades an increasing number of baby-boomer Americans got interested in East-Asian mysticism. Some even proclaimed themselves to be atheists. The fact remains, though, that they were born and raised in homes, and a society, that is based on Christianity. An "outsider" notices the idiosyncrasy.

Consider another culture. The contrast between a Western (Christian) culture and a Middle Eastern (essentially Muslim) culture is no more evident than when looking at religion.

In his book "The River War: An Historical Account of the Reconquest of the Soudan," Winston Churchill wrote: "Individual Muslims may show splendid qualities . . . . but the influence of [this] religion paralyzes the social development [sic] of those who follow it." This quote was taken from an October 12, 2009 NEWSWEEK article by Jeffrey Bartholet entitled: "It is a Mad, Mad, Mad, Mad World." Churchill fought jihadists in what is now Pakistan, then "fought the followers of the Mahdi at Omdurman, in Sudan," wrote Bartholet in his article.

In the late 19th century and the early 20th century, the U. K., and to a lesser extent, France occupied and controlled many countries in Africa, south east Asia and the Middle East. The British, and the French, had extensive physical presence in the countries under their rule.

Living among the citizens of the occupied territories enabled a good understanding and insight into such cultures. The above quote of Winston Churchill is but one example.

Until right after 9/11, the United States had no physical presence in a predominantly Muslim country.

As already mentioned, the author had lived for four decades in a predominantly Muslim culture with its own set of beliefs. The indelible effects religion could impart on a society are not hard to notice.

In a Muslim country, the whole culture is essentially the Islamic traditions. Such an underlying feature can be overlooked especially by a country that, correctly, prides itself on the separation between Church and State. But this is not the way a Muslim society operates.

On the positive side, the Islamic culture proved inhospitable, if not hostile, to communism and communist regimes. Apart from a short period of time, and mainly due to opposition to the West, Egypt never felt at ease dealing with the Soviet Union (The Russians invaded Afghanistan but the Afghans, with the United States help, drove them out in the late 1980s. Many Middle-Eastern Muslims left their countries to go fight side by side the Afghan Muslims against the Russians).

If anything, this tells how strong is the bond that Muslims feel toward each other—enough to leave one's own country to go fight in a foreign land only to help another Muslim whom he had never seen or known.

The same idea flows from a wide-spread social behavior.

Say, a Muslim got in an argument, fight or whatever conflict with a non-Muslim. It is the norm and accepted social behavior that any Muslim by-stander(s) should help the Muslim involved in the conflict to get the upper hand over the non-Muslim, regardless of whether the fighting Muslim was right or wrong.

That a Muslim helps another Muslim takes precedence over what is right or wrong! That is the thinking.

In Egypt, such antagonism toward non-Muslims is a rather recent phenomenon. Tolerance had characterized the Egyptian society for many years. But political developments in the Middle East during the second half of the 20th century altered the topography of the social arena.

Growing up in Egypt, the author, a Christian, recalls having many Muslim friends in the 1940s and the 1950s. Every one was aware of his/her religious identity but friendships and relationships crossed that barrier. Sometimes a Muslim accepted the invitation of a Christian friend to go to church on a Sunday. A Christian could share with his Muslim friend by fasting a day in the month of Ramadan (fasting from dawn till sunset).

But gradually the virus of intolerance started to spread, first regionally then globally.

An American friend told the author that in the 1960s the late President Nixon rightfully predicted that the 21st century would see the conflict between Christianity and Islam.

In addition to the opening to China, he, once again, proved to be right.

Some religious beliefs can have a profound impact on the social and even the economic welfare of a society. This may be especially true in a country like Egypt where religion is the main, if not the only, pillar of culture.

In Islam, a man can have up to four wives at the same time. At least theoretically, a person may have four wives, divorce one and then marry another one. This is religiously correct since he never exceeded having four wives at any particular time.

When the husband passes away leaving children from some, or possibly, each of his four, five or six wives—an extreme situation to be sure, but possible, complications follow. Most often than not, the heirs from even a single wife may not always like each other that much—the love of money is the root of much evil as the Bible says.

Now think about the heirs from a number of "competing" wives, each fighting for a bigger piece of the pie for herself and her children (wills are not common in Egypt).

Just like in marriage, divorce brings in some legitimate concerns. A husband may divorce his wife by sending her the relevant documents due to whatever reason the husband chooses.

This scenario could happen during a conversation, away from home, with a business partner, a friend or foe and the husband would say: If a certain matter is not resolved in such a way, I am going to divorce my wife.

Suddenly, and without any wrongdoing on her part, the wife get divorced. The husband may later change his mind and decide to remarry his wife. That is feasible the first, second and third time—that is, divorce then remarry the same woman three times.

But after the third time of divorce, the husband can not remarry her except after a certain arrangement. A "mohallel" must get involved to rectify the situation and render the remarriage religiously possible.

The three-time divorced wife must marry a "mohallel" for one night who then must divorce her so that she can remarry her husband. The "mohallel" must have intercourse during that night with the divorced wife.

If this is not degrading for a woman (and her husband), I do not know what else this would be.

It may be argued that this arrangement is intended as a deterrent for the husband to repeatedly divorce a wife. But the deterrent comes at an exorbitant price.

In divorce, the husband can simply send the divorce papers through an official to the wife who instantly becomes divorced. She has no input whatsoever.

If the husband later (within 40 days from divorce) changed his mind and decided to remarry his divorced wife but, for whatever reason, she did not want to, she can not refuse. If she did, the court issues a restraining order to force her into her husband's care. If he chooses, his obligation is only to rent for her a room, even on a roof, with nothing but a carpet on the floor and there she lives.

Talk about fairness and human dignity.

Only in 2005, Egypt allowed the wife to divorce her husband—it is called "El Khalgh" in Arabic. Note that it is not called "divorce" probably since divorce is the husband's privilege.

In such a social setting, the society's nucleus (the family) is shattered. The wife, and mother of children, has no security. She has no idea if and when her husband would divorce her. It is hard to blame the wife when she tries, by all means, to protect herself—her future as well as her children.

One common strategy is for the wife to get as many children as she could. This exhausts the husband's financial resources, and the chances are that he could not afford neither divorce her and pay child support for all these children, nor could he marry a second wife. The scheme sometimes work but at a great expense to the family and the society as a whole.

Another track that can bring in the same result of depleting the husband's income is to spend and spend, or put aside money behind his back. Children grow up and the feelings of insecurity carry over. And the cycle continues.

Now, the problem does not, logically, stop within the boundaries of the family. The sense of instability leads, inevitably, to distrust that takes precedence over all other considerations. It is just a natural defense mechanism.

As the saying goes: Me and my brother against my cousin; and me and my cousin against the stranger.

It goes without saying that if my immediate family fails to provide me an atmosphere of love, stability and, consequently, trust, then do not expect me to trust others whom I do not know.

The danger of distrust is that it is contagious. Once it is left to fester, it would be almost impossible to eradicate from society.

What makes distrust so detrimental to a culture is that it breeds other ills: suspicion, resentment, and even hatred. These negative forces could trammel progress as it consumes much needed human energy and time.

As the author had witnessed in a society where religion (Islam) makes divorce so handy, it tends to weaken or destroy the family and, therefore, a society.

Marriage is hard. It requires love and sacrifice—on both sides: the husband and the wife. But if the two approach marriage with divorce as an option, the marriage is likely to dissolve.

In the absence of divorce from the back of their mind, the two could find ways to overcome, and deal with, their differences (there will always be some points of conflict). As winners, they would benefit their children and, yes, the society as a whole.

An article in Wall Street Journal, March 9, 2011, p. A15 entitled: "How to Keep Going and Going," by Laura Landro reports on the book:The Longevity Project by Howard Friedman and Leslie Martin (Hudson Street Press). Landro wrote:

> " . . . . The respondents to the [eight decade] study who fared best in the longevity sweepstakes tended to have a fairly high level of physical activity, ... a thriving and long-running career, and a healthy marriage and family life. They summoned resilience against reverses and challenges—including divorce, loss of a spouse . . . . By contrast, those with the darkest dispositions . . . . were most likely to die sooner."

For the Christians in Egypt, the Church is the only institution that can divorce a married couple. If a married couple seeks, and attains, divorce in court, each is still considered married in the eyes of the church, and neither of them can remarry again since only the Church can officiate marriage.

The Church maintains an extremely tight cap on divorce allowing it only in exceptionally compelling situations, and after a high-ranking commission of the clergy study each case fastidiously.

In the U. S. it has been reported that 50 percent of marriages fail. Courts handle divorce cases for Christians as well as for those of other beliefs. Lisa Miller, in an article entitled: "Marriage is Hard. The religious right admits," NEWSWEEK, October 19, 2009, p. 25, reported that:

> "According to the Pew Forum, evangelicals are more likely to be divorced than Roman Catholics, Mormons, the Eastern Orthodox, Muslims, Jews, Hindus, and atheists . . . . the Institute for American Values . . . . found, not surprisingly, that the health of marriage in America is on the decline . . . . It's as true with Christians as it is with other religious groups."

What this really tells us is that, in the U. S., divorce has become a cultural phenomenon that transcends religious lines.

Whether the the above findings about the "health of marriage in America" were based on absolute numbers or percentages does not exonerate the Church.

Could the Churches have done more to protect the institution of marriage ? A tough question.

Could the Churches influence a culture or do they simply reflect values of a secular society?

What is clear, though, is that the negative impact of divorce is yet to be felt. Several factors may be helping to offset the problem: the high standard of living, a functional judicial system, and a culture that, only a few decades ago, was dominated by Christianity.

There are signs lately that divorce, as a trend, has reached its apex and is on the way down.

By contrast, in Islam marrying up to four, and the male dominance over decisions of divorce constitute major hurdles to the social wellbeing, but they are not the only strange and unique features. The following are some practices that illustrate the point.

Over the last few decades more and more females entered the workforce. Married female employees spend a considerable amount of time with male colleagues.

The chances of illicit relationships worried those responsible for protecting Islam.

To forbid such potential behavior, the Imams (Islamic clergy) recommended that the married female employee should breast-feed her colleague—the adult male. In this way they can not get married since she became as a "mother" to the man as a result of this act.

The reader may use his/her imagination to visualize an adult male being breast-fed by a female that could be of his age or even younger.

The phenomenon is called "breast feeding of the adult."

Another practice deals with dogs and pigs. Both are considered "unclean" by Muslims. This implies that eating pigs is forbidden.

In Egypt, a Christian called Mark had three stores that used to sell pork for Christians. After the last epidemic of influenza (the swine flu), the authorities closed the three stores, destroyed all the pigs and Egypt has no pork to this day.

Because dogs are "unclean," they are chased on the streets by children throwing rocks at them.

Before a Muslim prays, ablution is a must; the person must meticulously wash his/her hands up to the elbows, as well as the feet and genitals. If for any reason s/he touches a dog, all the washing must be redone. The same applies if a man just touches the hand of a woman.

Ablution is easily abolished and must be strictly followed.

As far as dogs are concerned, a female Muslim must not be seen naked by a male dog at home. And this is not a joke.

These "religious" practices (breast-feeding of the adult, a male dog should not be allowed to see a naked woman, ...) are claimed to be part of "Hadeeth"; a record of conversations between the prophet and those around him. Although "Hadeeth" is separate from Quraan, it is an authoritative document that is highly regarded as a foundation of Islamic teachings.

Lately, these practices had put fanatics on the defensive. Gone are the times when Imams held a firm grasp on what aspects of Islam, if any, are open for discussion. Undoubtedly, the Internet and social networking had extended the horizons of the ordinary Muslim especially the educated ones.

In a recent visit to Cairo, the author had the chance to read some articles in the widespread and semi-official newspaper of Al-Ahram. Some commentaries claim that "Hadeeth" is devoid of such teachings that have been falsely attributed to Islam.

To put fanatics on the defensive is no small matter. Enough to recall how rigid and self-righteous are Muslims about their religion to the point of strongly claiming that "Islam is the solution" to all the world problems.

The claim that such practices are not Islamic poses a question: who, when and how such notions have been added to "Hadeeth?"

Another practice may shed light on how Muslims approach their religion.

A woman can use nail polish so long as the film thickness of the polish does not exceed a certain value. A thicker layer of nail polish renders her ablution invalid. She must remove the polish first before performing ablution.

These instructions, as the author personally watched on TV, were according to the late Sheikh Al-Shaarawi—the most renowned Egyptian Imam during the 1970s, and beyond; the sheikh was well-known in all the Arab world.

In an Islamic culture, peer pressure is as profound as it can be—its social effects are dominant and can not be overlooked.

During the month of Ramadan, Muslims fast from dawn to sunset. During day time restaurants are closed. No one is expected to be seen eating or smoking in public—whether in the workplace, street, or public transportation. This is the norm and accepted social behavior. This does not necessarily mean that all Muslims do fast during Ramadan.

Only a negligible few dare to say no, or violate that in public. It takes a lot of confidence and courage for a Muslim to, say, smoke a cigarette in public (smoking is widespread in Egypt—in social gatherings one offers cigarettes to all present, then it is the turn of another person to do the offering, and so on).

In 1961 and 1962 the author remembers a Muslim faculty professor who used to smoke in the workplace during Ramadan.

Once Dr. El-Badry entered his office in the morning he would have a cup of Turkish coffee (strong, concentrated coffee prepared for him by the custodian). He was a heavy smoker and a cigarette hung from his lips uninterrupted until it was gone, to be replaced by a fresh one that was lighted from the previous cigarette.

Professor El-Badry was widely respected and much liked by his colleagues and his students.

But this was back in the early 1960s before the virus of fanaticism had the chance to infiltrate and contaminate the society.

A society with such a powerful influence of peer pressure would not, logically, allow for personal freedom or choice. Every Muslim must follow the Islamic traditions of fasting during Ramadan and praying five times a day. Ostracizing awaits those who dare to differ.

Praying at the mosque carries more "rewards" than praying at home. Going to the mosque to pray has the added "benefit" of having other Muslims recognize that you are faithful to your religion.

The Friday (holy day in Muslim countries) prayer in particular has a distinctive mark. It is not unusual to see big tents erected beside mosques on Friday to accommodate those who could not find a place inside. In the absence of a tent, carpets are extended on the streets close to the mosque.

Because Islamic religion is the culture's main pillar, and because no separation between religion and state exists in Egypt (and all other Muslim countries except Turkey for that matter), it is not uncommon to hear the Imam(s) talk about politics during the Friday speech that follows prayer. With the hearts, minds and ears open, Imams could convey the message in a way to instigate riots. This occurred on several occasions right after the Friday prayer.

Authorities in Egypt (and, I heard, Saudi Arabia) had to interfere to stop poisoning worshipers' minds with extreme, destructive ideologies.

A glimpse of hope for rapprochement between Islam and Christianity followed the election of Benedict XVI as the Pope of the Roman Catholic Church.

George Weigel wrote an article entitled: "How Benedict XVI Will Make History," published in the April 21, 2008 issue of NEWSWEEK, p. 38. Weigel said:

> ". . . . his Regensburg Lecture on faith and reason, ... on September 12, 2006, quoted a Byzantine emperor's sharp critique of Islam. Benedict XVI drew worldwide criticism. Others, however, including significant personalities in the complex worlds of Islam, took the Pope's point about the dangers of faith detached from reason quite seriously . . . . and . . . . there have been potentially historic tectonic shifts going on, both within Islam and in the world of inter religious dialogue."

Weigel went on to say that the Pope:

> "received two open letters from Muslim leaders . . . . [one] proposed a new dialogue between Islam and the Vatican . . . . through a Catholic-Muslim Forum that will meet twice yearly . . . . [to] address two issues that Benedict XVI has insisted be the focus of conversation: religious freedom, understood as a human right that everyone can grasp by reason, and the separation of religious and political authority in the modern state . . . ."

> "King Abdullah of Saudi Arabia visited Benedict XVI in November 2007. Subsequently, the king announced his own interfaith initiative . . . . and negotiations between the Holy See and Saudi Arabia opened on building the

first Catholic Church in the Kingdom. (A new Catholic Church, also the first of its kind, recently opened in Doha, Qatar.) . . . . Benedict XVI had made significant changes in the Vatican's intellectual approach to these volatile issues. Catholic veterans . . . . who did not press issues like religious freedom and reciprocity between the faiths have been replaced by scholars who believe that facing the hard questions helps support those Muslim reformers who are trying to find an authentic Islamic path to civility, tolerance, and pluralism. Thus Benedict XVI has quietly put his pontificate behind the forces of Islamic reform . . . ."

CHAPTER 21

STATUS OF WOMEN

For good or bad, we live in a male-dominated world. This may be true for all societies.

It follows, then, that the status of women in a culture is a reflection of men's view of them.

Religion is usually the well from which the human race seeks guidance, especially on such a compelling subject. After all, the woman is a wife, mother, daughter, or sister, and her role in raising children is beyond dispute. Today's children are tomorrow's leaders, and mothers have a lot to do with shaping their minds as well as their hearts. As the old saying goes: "The hand that rocks the cradle rules the world."

Christianity honors the woman. The Lord Jesus Christ was born of a virgin. The New Testament mentions many women who listened, loved, and believed in the Lord. The first person to see the empty tomb was a woman follower. The longest recorded conversation Jesus had with anyone was with the Samaritan woman.

The greatest honor Christianity bestows on women is evident from the sacredness of marriage. The man leaves his father and mother to marry; the husband and wife become one flesh.

Only adultery justifies divorce, according to the New Testament.

The Creator had laid down the teachings that are best for the family and, consequently, the society.

But not all religions share Christianity's view of woman.

Islam bestows great power on the man at the expense of the woman.

This is clear in marriage as well as in divorce (chapter 20).

The husband, at his sole discretion, can divorce and remarry up to four wives at a time.

It is crucial here to realize that a woman, even an educated woman with a professional career, has the natural, biological aspiration to marry and form a family. The role of having a family and raise children, in most cases, supersedes a woman's career if she has to choose. This may illustrate how marriage is tied up to a woman's view of life in a culture. When religion looks at the woman (wife) as a disposable object, family life is likely to suffer.

In Egypt, many Muslim wives envied Christian wives for the security they enjoy in marriage.

Some educated, strong-willed Muslim ladies raised voices of concern about the unfair treatment of women, especially in marriage. The second half of the 20th century has seen an exponential increase in the number of women with college degrees and post-graduate education. Many have had professional careers and some entered the political arena to share in the legislative process as members of the parliament.

During a visit to Egypt, in 2009, the author heard about some encouraging political developments. Some female representatives in the parliament tried to enact a law that limits the power of the husband and strengthens women's rights especially in the issue of marriage and divorce.

As stated earlier, we live in a male-dominated world. The parliament, with a majority of men, defeated the proposed legislation. Any thought that would deprive a man of some of his power would face an uphill battle. Those who opposed the legislation claimed their religious right (from the Quraan) to divorce and marry more than one wife, simultaneously.

But this was a start. There have been some expressions of opposition to the status of women in Egyptian society as expressed in the media, and even in some movies. However, the ultimate change would come when concerns are transformed into legislation that becomes the law of the land.

There are certainly some forces that are helping to push in the right direction.

The Internet and satellites are foremost. The first enabled a personal, and largely uncensored window on the outside world, while the second provided an opportunity to send and receive audible and video messages instantly (recall the cell-phone-transmitted picture of the young Iranian lady beaten to death on the streets of Tehran in 2009 while protesting the regime of the Mullahs).

The Internet, one of the most versatile inventions of the human mind, had contributed immensely to the worldwide spread of knowledge. This is crucial particularly in those areas where there is some degree of censorship on the flow of information. Censorship is not necessarily a government-imposed phenomenon. In some cultures, certain topics are taboo. Social censorship can be as powerful as, if not more restrictive than, a government-imposed one.

The Islamic culture does not condone questions which attempt to address a practice that has proved time and again to be of negative impact.

Womens' rights is a case in point. It goes without saying that most, if not all, Muslim women disapprove of the religion's practice that gives total power to the husband to divorce and to marry up to four wives—at a time. But to publicly criticize the practice requires a considerable amount of courage and self-confidence. That is why it is encouraging to hear about an attempt, even an unsuccessful one, to change such an unfair and socially-destructive behavior.

Peer pressure is extremely powerful in an Islamic culture. The subtle forces of peer pressure (fasting in Ramadan, divorce, polygamy, . . .) exert an enormous impact on the culture and society.

To put things in perspective, consider the Islamic culture in countries other than Egypt.

Islam exists predominantly in North Africa, the Middle East, South and Southeast Asia. Over all, the cultures are Islamic. But there is a wide spectrum that describes present-day practices throughout these areas.

At one extreme is Turkey. In the 1920s, Kamal Atatürk shifted the culture away from being Islamic to a more or less Western-style society. (Over the last few years, however, the ruling political party has exhibited signs of retracting probably as a reaction to opposition by the European Union for accepting Turkey as a full member.)

At the other extreme are countries like Afghanistan and probably Yemen.

Others fall in between with varying degrees of social development that is essentially proportional to exposure to Western culture.

Iran and Egypt adapted well till 1979 when the Shah was overthrown by the Mullahs, and Egypt had a setback that was not abrupt but gradual. Internal strong forces of extremism are playing in Egypt but the government is alert and walking a tightrope to keep the country safe, but not completely alienating the jihadists.

To illustrate: Egyptian ladies (Muslims and Christians) like to dress fashionably. The European style was popular till the 1980s when the "hejab" started to appear on Cairo streets. The phenomenon spread like a cancer. Now you can walk on the street and identify female Muslims from those who are Christians by the way they dress: the first wear hejab, the Christians dress normally as they always did. Even girls in grade school cover their heads. The change has been gradual but can not be mistaken.

In spite of the negative forces that are trying to pull Egypt backwards, it fares better than say Afghanistan—as if one should feel content and happy about that.

Aryan Baker (TIME, August 9, 2010, p. 20) reported a quite disturbing incident from Kabul:

> "The Taliban pounded on the door just before midnight, demanding that Aisha, 18, be punished for running away from her husband's house. They dragged her to a mountain clearing near her village . . . . ignoring her protests that her in-laws had been abusive, that she had no choice but to escape. Shivering in the cold air and blinded by the flashlights trained on her by her husband's family, she faced her spouse and accuser. Her

> in-laws treated her like a slave . . . . They beat her . . . . Her judge, a local Taliban commander, was unmoved. Later, he would tell Aisha's uncle that she had to be made an example of lest other girls . . . . try to do the same thing . . . . Aisha's brother-in-law held her down while her husband pulled out a knife. First he sliced off her ears. Then he started on her nose. Aisha passed out from the pain . . . . The men had left her on the mountainside to die . . . . It (the story) happened last year. Now hidden in a secret women's shelter in the relative safety of Kabul, where she was taken after receiving care from U. S. forces, Aisha recounts her tale . . . ."

Aisha's face with the mutilated nose appeared on the cover of TIME.

In the same article Baker went further to say:

> " . . . . the Taliban will be advocating a version of an Afghan state in line with their own conservative views particularly on the issue of women's rights, which they deem a Western concept that contravenes Islamic teaching . . . . In rural areas, a family that finds itself shamed by a daughter sometimes sells her into slavery, or worse, subject her to a so-called honor killing—murder under the guise of saving the family's name."

Honor killing is not restricted to Afghanistan, though.

Upper (southern) Egypt has known the phenomenon for quite some time but the practice had abated as the society progressed over the years—at least through education.

So, here are two countries (Afghanistan and Egypt) which share a line of thinking that can not be attributed to geographic location, as they are separated by thousands of miles. The common thread is the Islamic culture and how it values women.

The difference between the two societies is only a matter of degree. Afghanistan has remained isolated from the world (the

British and the Soviets have not stayed long enough to exert any social change), whereas Egypt has always been in contact with the outside world.

Cultural changes, especially involving customs tied to religion, can not be enforced by foreign powers but may be allowed to develop slowly on their own. The Internet and the media are powerful tools that slowly but surely can bring about some desirable results.

In Egypt, privately-owned TV stations broadcast uncensored. A couple of these stations show only Christian programs. The effect, though minimized if not flatly denied, is felt as some Muslims convert to Christianity. In a Muslim-dominated culture, such conversions have rarely, if ever, occurred before the Internet and satellite broadcasting. These outlets enabled privacy for the inquisitive minds to know about Christianity—a taboo in an Islamic society.

Another aspect of women's inferiority in the Islamic culture is exhibited in the area of inheritance.

In Egypt, for example, a son inherits double the daughter's share. Such practice is lawful and is enforced on both Muslims and Christians. To circumvent such an unfair practice, some Christians include the names of sons and daughters as equal owners on the deed of a property when purchased.

CHAPTER 22

ISLAMIC CULTURE AND DEMOCRACY

According to Webster's dictionary, democracy is: "government by the people, either directly or through elected representatives; the acceptance and practice of the principle of equality of right, opportunity and treatment."

In the West, democracy has flourished. Democratic institutions have been well established. The system had generally produced prosperous, peaceful and productive societies. Not always perfect but functionally-proven ones.

The author can not help but think that the basis of democracy (Webster's definition above) is deeply rooted in Christianity. We believe that God had created people equally with unalienable rights. Which is to say that people enjoy freedom, liberty, and pursuit of happiness not as a gift from the government but as bestowed by God upon His creation.

> Amendment XIV of the U. S. Constitution states that: " . . . . nor shall any State deprive any person of life, liberty, or property, without due process of law; nor deny to any person within its jurisdiction the equal protection of the laws."

For more than two centuries, the Constitution has been followed, respected and executed as the Founders intended it to be. Even in extreme political and national security issues when it seems so tempting, and even justifiable, to shift away from the Constitution, strong voices are raised against the trespassing. The Constitution always prevailed.

The crucial point is not just having a Constitution, but safeguarding against any attempt to sidestep it. One wonders how many other countries do have some sort of a Constitution that is selectively applied, or even modified, to serve those who happen to be in power.

It can safely be theorized that democracy entails tolerance (of different ideas and beliefs) and pluralism (all citizens regardless of their background, race, ethnicity, country of origin, religion, ...).

Then, what about a culture that is essentially based on intolerance and single-mindedness? Could it be reconciled to democracy? Could a culture that believes Islam is the only solution to all world problems be receptive to any other ideas? Could a culture that regards those who do not believe in Islam to be infidels treats its citizenry equally? Could a culture held captive to the thought that Islam is the only correct religion live in peace and harmony with those who do not believe in Islam? Could a culture that pressures even its non-adherents to fast in Ramadan tolerate non-Muslims?

One might argue that there are non-Muslims who are citizens of countries with Muslim majorities. That is true.

But are infidels looked upon and treated equally in those countries? Are they welcome or just an annoyance that the society has to live with? Are they considered to be loyal citizens or that their loyalty is always in question?

The two previous chapters (20 and 21) talked about features of an Islamic culture. It should not be hard to realize how restrictive such a culture could be.

All Muslims are expected to follow the Islamic teachings without questioning. They should fast the month of Ramadan, and pray five times a day . . . .

In the area of the family, however, the culture is so permissive to the point of hurting the nucleus of society; the husband can easily divorce his wife at his sole discretion, and marry up to four wives at a time. Attempts to remedy the practice have been rejected out-of-hand.

It has been claimed that Islam is good for "all" places at "all" times. One can only wonder: In recent times when a high percentage of females are highly educated, is it appropriate not to have any input from the wife regarding termination of her marriage? Many a Muslim wife resent the implication, and a few men agree, but again the peer pressure ensures conformity.

The enormous powers of peer pressure in Islamic culture are unmistakable for anyone who has lived in such societies. A culture that is characterized by intolerance of any ideas that do not fit its mold can not accept democracy as a way of life. A culture that sees one correct path to heaven can not be a pluralistic society. It may be futile to try otherwise.

The Wall Street Journal (Saturday/Sunday, March 6/7, 2010, p. A13) reported on the conversion of Mosab Hassan Yousef (32) from Islam to Christianity.

The converted Muslim is the son of a founder and leader of Hamas. Matthew Kaminski wrote:

> " . . . . a British cabbie in Jerusalem . . . . gave him an English-Arabic copy of the New Testament and invited him to attend a Bible study session. Mosab Yousef in his book "Son of Hamas," says: I found that I was really drawn to the grace, love and humility that Jesus talked about. What was the reaction? Kaminski asked. Sheikh Yousef (his father) issued a statement that he and his family have completely disowned the man who was our oldest son. The son (Mosab) says:The problem is not in Muslims. The problem is with their God. They need to be liberated from their God. He is their biggest enemy. It has been 1,400 years they have been lied to. Mosab says: he is not afraid about his life. Is he in danger? Most likely he is."

Talk about tolerance even between a father and his son.

Consider the recent (2009 and 2011) events on the Egyptian soil where Christians have been attacked and killed as they left the church service on January 7 (Christmas eve) at Nagagh Hammadi, and on New Year's eve at Alexandria, respectively.

Are these actions the fruit of a peaceful, tolerant religion as some claim it to be?

After the toppling of Saddam Hussein's regime in Iraq, there was hope in establishing a new political system that would be a model of democracy in the region. The last few years may have proved otherwise.

In Islamic cultures, Islam encompasses all aspects of life: political, social and economic.

To change the political system from dictatorship to democracy one may have to look at the underlying culture. Is it open to new ideas? Is it capable and willing to accommodate people of different beliefs and origins?

The inherent forces of peer pressure in an Islamic culture causes a question to spring to mind: If the culture does not mix well with democracy, does it help breed dictatorships?

If the answer is no, why then are most Islamic societies governed by, varying degrees of, dictatorship regimes?

If history tells us something, it is that dictatorships are short-lived—they run on assumptions that are contrary to the intrinsic human forces of freedom.

Then "suddenly" came the Uprising of January 25, 2011 in Egypt.

But why "suddenly?"

In TIME (February 14, 2011, p. 26), Fareed Zakaria wrote:

> "Egypt has long been seen as a society deferential to authority, with a powerful state and a bureaucracy that might have been backward and corrupt but nonetheless kept the peace. Zakaria quotes Fouad Ajami's essay of 1995 in which he said: This is a country with a remarkable record of political stability . . . . in the past two centuries, Egypt has been governed by just two regimes, a monarchy

> set up in 1805 and the Free Officers Movement that came to power in 1952 with Gamal Abdel Nasser . . . . In the popular imagination, Egyptians are passive, meekly submitting to religion and hierarchy. But by the end of January the streets of Cairo and Alexandria and other cities were filled with a different people: crowds of energetic, strong-willed men from all walks of life and even some women, all determined to shape their destiny and become masters of their own fate."

The world was surprised by what took place lately in Egypt—first in Cairo then at other locations whether within Egypt or in the region. As one protester put it: Egyptians surprised themselves.

Egypt has historically been at the heart of the Middle East (Chapter 3). The recent events reveal that she still is.

Since the assassination of the late president Anwar El-Sadat, in 1981, his vice president at the time, Husni Mubarak, used the emergency laws to govern Egypt. Was it justified? Probably so if one considers the fact that Sadat was assassinated by members of an Islamic organization (Muslim Brotherhood or an offshoot) that managed to smuggle live ammunition for some assault rifles carried by soldiers parading in front of the reviewing stand.

Shortly after the military revolution of 1952, it became a common practice to have a military parade every year. All weapons parading were devoid of live ammunition. The success in breaking this strict, long-established rule attested to the power of the Islamic fundamentalists who could infiltrate the armed forces at such a critical moment.

To his credit, Mubarak maintained a watchful eye on these extremists.

But as it is usually the case: It may not be easy to find the right balance between what is reasonable and what is excessive.

To maintain Egypt's safety from those who intended harm (even if those elements saw otherwise) was a desirable goal, but to extend punishment to human rights activists, and torture those who were imprisoned went overboard.

Was it Mubarak's orders, or the cronies who aspired to please the higher-ups? In either case, the damage was done.

After the military came to power in 1952, General Naguib was a figurehead and soon Nasser became the president. He had Sadat as his vice president. When Nasser passed away, Sadat became the president till his assassination when Mubarak, his vice president, took the presidency. So this was the logical sequence.

But Mubarak had no vice president—for 30 years. He had been grooming his son, Gamal, to be the next president of Egypt. Gamal was the head of the ruling National Democratic party—the most powerful political party. Rumors about his son as the next president have been circulating for many years.

Did Egypt reverse its system from being a republic to a monarchy? It is true that Assad (the father) had his son become the president of Syria about a decade ago, but the precedent had no legs. The families of Assad and Mubarak lacked the legitimacy of a bona fide monarchy.

But for Mubarak to plan to have his son become the next president, or to rule under emergency laws with an iron fist that tended to shift toward brutality were not, in the author's opinion, the main motivation behind the uprising.

The January 25 uprising was primarily driven by economic reasons. As John Negroponte, the director of National Intelligence in the Bush administration, expressed it in a CNN interview with Candy Crowley: Egypt has a lot of smart and educated people.

Many college graduates are out of work. Although the Egyptian economy has been growing by 6.5 percent over the past five years or so, the average citizen has not seen any gains, yet. It has been said that it takes 15 years for the citizenry to see improvements.

Fareed Zakaria (TIME, February 14, 2011) calls the attention to "a phenomenon that political scientists have dubbed: a revolution of rising expectations. Dictatorships find it difficult to handle change because the structure of power they have set up cannot respond to the new, dynamic demands coming from their people."

Food prices have been rising uncontrollably especially over the past decade. A long, hot summer in 2010 did a lot of damage to vegetable crops. Rumors abound about corruption at the highest levels.

The ill-conceived housing policies of the 1950s and 1960s exacerbated the agony. The lucky few who could land a job were confronted by an unsurmountable obstacle of finding a place to live in, marry, and have a family. Just the normal expectations.

Many Egyptians had to leave Egypt to look for work opportunities. In addition to trying at the neighboring Arab countries, some had to ride small boats that smuggle them to Greece or Italy only to be arrested and deported.

Talk about humiliation.

But was the economy and corruption the only factors that aided the uprising to continue? There are strong suspicions that the Muslim Brotherhood was operating behind the scene. The organization has long been known to be well organized and ready to step in once the circumstances became favorable. They are trying to alleviate fears from them by claiming to be an inclusive group that aspires to treat every body equally—including the minority Christians. If history is any guide, such promises are hard to believe in.

Fareed Zakaria (TIME, February 14, 2011) points out that:

> "When the Pew Research Center surveyed the Arab world last April . . . . 82% of Egyptians support stoning as a punishment for adultery, 84% favor the death penalty for Muslims who leave the religion, and in the struggle between modernizers and fundamentalists, 59% identify with fundamentalists."

But Zakaria cites results from another Pew survey.

> "A 2007 poll found that 90% of Egyptians support freedom of religion, 88% an impartial judiciary and 80% free speech; 75% are opposed to censorship, and, according to the 2010 report, a large majority believes that democracy is preferable to any other kind of government."

Two surveys run in the short span of three years, yet there seems to be some conflicting results. In 2007, 90% of Egyptians support freedom of religion, but in 2010, 84% favor the death penalty for Muslims who leave the religion. Does this mean: A Muslim is free to leave his religion but will suffer the death penalty for that? What type of freedom this leads to? Religious dictatorship?

In statistics, it is known that phrasing the question might influence the answer and hence the poll results. It may be safe to assume that the questions used in the two surveys were carefully phrased. Did the respondents chose their answers accurately, or were the answers selected because they represented a popular idea—such as "freedom of religion?"

In talking about the recent uprising in Egypt, one can not overlook the role of technology.

When the Internet was invented in the 1990s, no one could have then dreamed that the social media (Facebook, Twitter, Blogs) would serve as the main tool in organizing the masses.

Undemocratic societies with limited, or no, freedom of the press are deprived the means of feeling the social pulse—members of the community have no means of communicating with each other. Anger builds up when it has no legitimate avenues to express itself.

In a recent visit to Egypt, in October 2010, a relative described the mood of the Egyptian people as quite angry and on the verge of explosion.

When a few thousands showed up in Tahrir (Liberation) square in the morning of January 25, they were gathered through a Facebook website that apparently had specified the date and place. Soon thereafter, hundreds of thousands poured in the streets. People had already reached the boiling point. A spark was all what is needed for the ignition.

Iran, Algeria, Bahrain, Syria, Libya, and Yemen followed. Which protests would succeed and which would be subdued? Time would tell.

For Egypt, what would the outcome be?

Will the Armed Forces remain united, or that internal struggles could emerge taking the country on a dark road? Would the uprising lead to a democratic transition with a fair election of the Parliament and a president? Would the army then retreat to the barracks and let a civilian government rule? The army enjoyed a number of privileges since 1952—high salaries, excellent benefits, best hospitals, lucrative jobs on retirement from service, and private clubs. Would they forfeit such benefits? Not an easy decision.

And what about the powerful Muslim Brotherhood with its deep roots? Would they be content with a piece of the pie? Or would they strive to usurp all power after having a figurehead at the early stages of the process who would easily be removed at a later stage?

All are open questions with answers that are anyone's guess.

On February 12, 2011, CNN showed Egyptians sweeping the streets in and around Tahrir square after 18 days of protesting during which hundreds of thousands of people "lived" in tents erected in the square, and many slept on the ground. On February 14 the TV showed Egyptians doing street repairs and painting curbs.

The significance here can be felt from the comments made by some protesters who, in effect, said: This is our country and we are getting it back.

As an Egyptian-American who lived in Egypt for 40 years, the author could sense a new meaning that tended to disappear from the vocabulary of the citizenry over the past few decades.

Totalitarian regimes succeed in alienating their people who feel helpless with no input whatsoever in the affairs of their country.

The peaceful demonstrations were a testimony to the nature of the Egyptian people. Apart from the thugs who appeared in the square on February the 2nd, and the ensuing fights between the pro- and anti-government groups, and considering the scale and duration of protesting, it can safely be claimed that the demonstrations were peaceful.

A bright spot was the absence of any anti-American sentiments such as burning flags or accusatory, hostile signs. Actually many protesters expressed eagerness for more support from America. It looked as if protesters had in their mind the American values of freedom and democracy.

There is a great hope that what did not work in Iraq would work in Egypt.

CHAPTER 23

GEOGRAPHIC LIMITATIONS, INDIVIDUALISM, LANGUAGE, AND COMMUNICATION

Since the dawn of civilization, communities sought and settled around water resources. The Nile River in Egypt runs longitudinally from the south (border with Sudan) to the north (the Mediterranean Sea).

Life is still concentrated on the banks of the Nile, which forms a delta extending from Cairo northwards. The population increased from about 20 million in the 1950s to more than77 million as of January 2010, Dr. Abd-El-Monem Said reported in Al-Ahram, the Egyptian Newspaper, November 1st, 2010, p. 11 (in Arabic).The area of farmland (four percent of the total area of 386,000 square miles) remained essentially unchanged.

The High Dam at Aswan, built in the 1960s, did not meet the high expectations of increasing the agricultural wealth of the country. Egypt, an agricultural society, used to export wheat but now imports most of its needs of wheat as well as other crops.

The exponential increase in population (birth control is forbidden in Islamic societies) could not be met with any significant increase in the area of cultivated land. Industry languished.

The inevitable effect was double whammy. Inflation is uncontrollable, and the population density has reached unacceptable limits. Now, Cairo is said to have 20 million people. One neighborhood

(Shubra) in Cairo has more than 2.5 million—the population of the whole State of Kansas.

But there is hope. Two ideas are now under serious discussion to address these economic and social issues. Both ideas agree on the necessity of having a new "corridor" in the Western Desert. It will run parallel to, but far from, the Nile. Some advocate building the roads and other infrastructure first to be followed by the cities, whereas others believe that establishing the cities should be first; then come the roads and infrastructure.

Whatever the experts would decide, the idea is overdue.

In the meantime, crowding had its inevitable consequences. With a shortage in housing, the result of some misguided policies in the 1960s, extended families were forced to live together. A son or daughter who got married sometimes has to share the living space with the parents. The result is more tension that is, logically, carried over to the society. Anxiety predominates.

On top of that comes the perpetual hefty increase in the price of all products, services, and utilities. People are not particularly happy (Chapter 22). They may tell jokes and laugh, but this could only be a way to unburden the feeling of helplessness. Some say that without laughing, people could have "exploded" out of anger and frustration.

Crowding does not allow much room for privacy and individualism.

Egyptians tend to cluster together. Families and extended families tend to live as close to each other as they possibly could. A landlord would assign an apartment to each of his married sons and daughters. This is what the author's late father did, and my brother-in-law had followed suit. The practice carries two advantages. It keeps the family close, and also eliminates the possible headaches from some undesirable tenants.

To have families near to each other provides a rich social life and a sense of security, but tends to create problems nevertheless.

As long as there is a human being, there is always friction, as Dr. Charles Stanley said.

Now, an interesting question imposes itself: What is better 1. to have big families living close to each other and endure the associated struggles due to this closeness, or 2. have families spread apart but suffer loneliness, especially at later stages of life?

Each of the two alternatives has advantages and disadvantages. It probably boils down to what the society offers and agrees upon as the norm.

We grew up in a society that believes in, and encourages, families to be near so we tend to accept that as a way of life. Those who grew up in the U. S. may regard this as odd; the population density is low, and job opportunities usually require relocation away from the family. It has been said that the average American moves five to six times in a life time, and changes career three to four times. A dynamic society.

The cultural response to the reality of geographic limitations is evident in other societies as well.

Consider Japan (180 million). A group of volcanic islands with a limited area of inhabitable land. The result is a relatively high population density. The society is close knit. Neighbors know each other well.

The Egyptians are sociable and hospitable; a feature that has been noticed by visitors (not tourists) who had the opportunity to live in the country for some time.

To have a guest at home for a meal, the host and hostess show their hospitality by offering and even insisting that the visitor must try this or that. This is the normal and accepted social behavior. It would be a lack of generosity to do otherwise. The food always stays on the table; the hostess stands up and asks for the guest's plate, serves the food, and hands the plate back to the visitor. This is done to each guest.

Being hospitable is a natural behavior that transcends economic and/or social status of the family. A family of moderate means is as generous as a well-to-do one—relatively speaking. Actually the less fortunate could be more hospitable, as if trying to show that they are no less than anyone else. People have great dignity.

If someone gets sick, it is expected that family and friends check on him/her by a visit or a phone call. So long as the person remains ill, others should keep inquiring. People talk freely about their health problems. Sharing others in their difficult times, that is to sympathize with them, makes life more tolerable. It helps balance the unfavorable economic and social circumstances.

The rather tough conditions of life, expected in a developing country such as Egypt, can have a positive side effect. Empathy between most people is, or was, the norm.

During high-school years, the author recalls spending some summer days at his father's clinic. In many cases, the prescription written to the patient had only one medication. Asking my father why just prescribe one medication whereas three or four could ensure a cure, he would say: "my diagnosis is that the patient needs only this medication; additional ones could only add to the financial burden of a patient who apparently could not afford it" (at the time, Egypt had no health insurance).

One sometimes wonders whether hospitality, sociability, and empathy are the reasons why extended families tend to stick together, or that those features have developed as a result of some forced living circumstances? A tough question.

Tied up to being sociable is the tendency of the Egyptians to talk, and joke. Not all Arabic-speaking societies share this phenomenon. So, it is not linguistic. The author had been to Iraq and Oman to note the difference. Whereas the Egyptians and Omanis are peaceful, the Iraqis are violence-prone.

Does geographic limitations (population density) affect communication? Does it follow that societies with high population density tend to communicate more often? Probably so.

Living in the U. S. where population density is low, especially in most of the Midwest, it strikes the author how limited the communication is. Some subjects, such as religion and politics, are taboo. For men, sports and the weather are favorites; ladies find more subjects to talk about.

The author is a great admirer of the English language. It can convey the content in short, up-to-the point sentences.

This stands in contrast to the Arabic language that, besides hyperbole, tends to express itself in rather lengthy expressions.

Exaggeration is a built-in feature of the Arabic language. Even before the advent of Islam to the Arab peninsula in the seventh century, it was not uncommon that people addressed each other with poem. Such was the eloquence.

The pre-Islamic age (El-Asr El-Gahely, in Arabic) saw an abundance of poets and poetry. A poet may describe his sweetheart to be as beautiful as the moon (a symbol of beauty) and as slim as a deer (a symbol of elegance) even though she may be heavy set and far from being fair!

Strong emotions, and the exaggeration thereof, also expresses itself in attacking others—individuals or countries.

After the advent of Islam, a Muslim leader addressed the Iraqis saying: "Ya ahl El Iraq, ya ahl el kofr wal nefak, inny ara roosa kad ainat wa hana ketafea wa inni la katifiha." He was, in effect, saying: You Iraqis are known for disbelief and double-face talk. I [he] see that some heads are ripe for beheading, and I [he] intend to execute them.

So, most of those who have Arabic as their native tongue are consciously or subconsciously programmed to strongly express their opinions and, more often than not, in an exaggerated form.

Because language is one of the cultural features of a society, it may be imperative for an outsider to think of "exaggeration" in weighing statements coming out from Arabic-speaking societies.

To illustrate. In the 1960s Egypt had Mohammed H. Haikal, as the most popular and well-known journalist at the time presiding over the official, oldest (first issue on August 5th, 1876), and most widespread newspaper—till today. He wrote an article in Al-Ahram about this phenomenon and how it interacts with the political environment.

The article attributed the rhetoric that dominated the region prior to the 1967 war to such "exaggeration." Haikal said that when the media talked about "throwing the enemy in the sea," it did not literally mean that, but was simply expressing the feelings in its own cultural way. At the time a state of war provided a cloud of animosity over the whole region but the way this was exhibited and perceived made the difference. This was in the late 1960s, though.

Opinions may differ about this interpretation and whether it justified some of the rhetoric.

But the succeeding political developments lend some credibility to such a point of view.

Just a decade after the manifestation of the strongest expression of disagreement between Egypt and Israel, a peace treaty was signed between the two countries following the surprise visit to Israel by the late president of Egypt.

Did the change in power at the highest level in Egypt contribute to the new situation? Definitely so.

As previously stated, the English language stands in great contrast to the Arabic one. The practicality and to-the-point way of expression of English-speaking societies can not be mistaken. To put it differently: In English you say precisely what you mean—in Arabic what is said may or may not reflect the exact feelings of the speaker.

Another feature of Arabic-speaking societies is posturing and grandstanding. A trait of the human race, posturing is alive and well in almost every society though with varying degrees.

Regionally, the late President Nasser was instrumental in calling for the Arab countries to carry out their responsibilities toward the Palestinians. It is no secret that Egypt, and the Egyptians, paid more than their fair share in this regard. The negative consequences of a number of successive regional wars were clearly felt in the country—lives lost, military equipment that needed to be replenished, and a dysfunctional infrastructure. Let alone the debilitating impact on morale.

Yet it was not uncommon to hear voices from neighboring countries claiming that Egypt was not doing enough for the "Arab cause." They provided suggestions and unsolicited advice as to what needed to be done, not by their own countries but, by Egypt!

After the late President Sadat's visit to Israel in 1977 and the signing of the Peace Treaty in 1978, Egypt was publicly condemned as the "traitor," by almost all Arab countries.

Egyptians who had no chance but to go to the oil-rich countries looking for jobs were poorly treated. As an agricultural society the Egyptians have always felt tied up to their land—they never aspired to move away. The country paid a high price that had never seemed to satisfy the spectators sitting on the fence just posturing about their "contributions in defense of the Palestinians."

The whole region suffered from "El-Mozayadat", the Arabic word for grandstanding.

Posturing does not seem to be only political but social as well. Individual posturing is not uncommon.

The Egyptians, though friendly, are competitive, but only between themselves. Competitiveness could be a wellspring of achievement and success for the individual as well as for the society. But, 1.the path that competitiveness takes, and 2.the environment in which it works seem to impact the results, as discussed below.

1. The path of a healthy competitiveness encourages all involved to put the utmost of their effort in study, work, business or whatever the endeavor is. A largely positive outcome may logically be expected as every individual pour all of his/her energy in a productive way that benefits the individual and, in doing so, benefits the whole society.

This is not the path of competitiveness in Egypt where the phenomenon had apparently shifted from being constructive into being destructive. Egyptians do not feel comfortable with another person better than them. It does not matter whether the other person is a relative, close friend, colleague or a neighbor. Every person tries to impress the others around him/her by consciously or subconsciously pretending to be richer, more powerful, more knowledgeable or better-connected. This is exhausting as it saps human energy into fruitless battles.

In the hard economic times that had engulfed the country during the past several decades, such misguided competitiveness did not help. It converted a friendly society into a hostile one, and a positive feature was sadly lost.

2. The environment for a successful competitiveness should allow legitimate means and opportunities for those who are willing and ambitious. Strong legislative institutions and an

independent judiciary branch of government guarantee the rights of every body regardless of who they are or whom they know.

Such an integrated system takes time to be fully implemented.

Egypt, a developing country that had lately been distracted by a number of military conflicts, is trying to reestablish itself as a successful democracy. To maintain the momentum, however, a number of impeding forces have to be overcome.

On the negative side of the Egyptian culture, distrust stands out. Both social (chapter 20) and political (chapter 19) realities contributed.

Citizens have little trust in their government. But then one might ask: Who constitutes the government? If the government does not trust its citizens could it simply be because citizens do not trust each other?

Imagine a society in which the government does not trust its citizens, and the citizens do not trust their government—or each other.

The consequences are not hard to fathom. Paralysis is the logical outcome, and paralysis does have its powerful grip on the society.

For any meaningful national progress to occur, a minimum level of trust and stability must be maintained to provide a safety blanket for the risk takers to invest their capital. Lately, many policies have been under revision, and the country managed to attract foreign investments from Europe, Japan and the United States. The country can certainly do much better, though.

A case in point. Since the late 1950s factories have been built to assemble (not manufacture) cars. Fiat was the first, and others have followed suit. But, six decades later, the situation is unchanged—just assembling, no manufacturing.

As individuals the people are hard working, smart, innovative, and persistent. Successful Egyptians have proven themselves in the United States and several other societies where they live and work.

It may not be easy to pinpoint why the same individuals could be productive in a foreign society but not in their own?

Could it be due to some prevailing cultural forces that are dragging everyone down? Could it be the distrust, posturing and misguided competitiveness, favoritism, intolerant religion, women's status? All of the above?

Dr. Gaber Asfour, the renowned Egyptian literary critic, addressed the present crisis of the Egyptian culture in a recent article in Al-Ahram Newspaper issue of October 25, 2010, p.12. The article, in Arabic, was entitled: "The Egyptian Culture in a Crisis." To translate:

> "The Egyptian culture suffers a crisis that it has never faced before whether in its complexity or diversity, and it is breeding consequences in economics, industry and politics; areas that appear disconnected to culture but in reality are directly affected and influenced by it."

Professor Asfour, a Muslim, goes on to say that the culture of a nation affects all aspects of society from moral behavior to all values and traditions that in turn become forces of progress or decline.

The first aspect of Egyptian culture Asfour discusses is the status of women (see also chapter 21). He reiterates how the 1919 revolution liberated the woman symbolically by abolishing the "hejab." The social progress of women took a jolt and continued thereafter at least till the end of the 1960s.

Asfour wonders what happened to that woman whether concerning her progress or how she is perceived by society and even her own self image? He cites questions submitted by females to Islamic TV channels that help spread religious ignorance. Questions about if she can undress in front of a male dog in the house? Should the woman enter the bathroom with the left or right foot? What about the famous "breast feeding of the adult?"

"The Egyptian woman now refuses to elect women candidates to local councils or to the parliament."

Dr. Asfour wrote: "What happened was a retreat of the society's image about the woman; her awareness of herself declined to the extent that the woman became an obstacle to her own progress—as if the women have collaborated with men whose social awareness keep retreating trying to get the woman backwards by keeping her busy with the hejab of the mind before hejab of the face.

Asfour wonders if the women who called for taking the hejab off a century ago would have dreamed that the Egyptian woman would be pulled back to the hejab under the disguise of morality? He continues:

> "The backward culture brought in more of the same, and led to a state of crisis. The forms of political and economic retreat added to the religious rigidity to strengthen the inherited backward culture, and renders it more bleak. The present Egyptian culture had replaced the freedom of speech and expression with remnants of the emergency law and extremist Imams who keep intimidating the civic intelligentsia to push them back too."

> "The cultural crisis has many features, one of which is religious extremism on both sides: Muslims and Christians. Such extremism runs parallel to a rigidity in critical thinking that does not allow for a difference in opinion—those who dare to differ are accused of being traitors or agents of the regime."

Dr. Asfour blames the State for absence of serious social dialogue, and not including the citizen in making some major decisions.

> "Egyptians do not see a trace for the right of citizens for expression, health insurance, political and democratic practices in the midst of all the corruption and favoritism. We speak about human rights but in reality these rights are trespassed upon, and, sadly, the citizen does not know what are these rights."

Such an insight is coming from a Muslim who is highly educated, a literary critic, and a veteran who had seen Egypt going from a prosperous, democratic, secular society to one with a struggling economy, limited freedoms, and intolerant religious extremism.

CHAPTER 24

PROSPERITY AND ITS BY-PRODUCTS

In chemistry, scientists distinguish between two basic types of reactions: inorganic and organic.

Consider the general reaction:

$$A + B = C + D$$

If the reactants A and B are inorganic (basically a salt of a metal such as iron, silver, or lead . . . . , reacting with a nonmetallic compound containing a halogen, oxygen, nitrogen, ...), the reaction is an inorganic reaction. It is virtually instantaneous, and yields 100 percent of C and D, with no by-products.

On the other hand, if the reactants A and B contain carbon, and hydrogen as the main constituents, the reaction is classified as an organic reaction.

This type of reactions is characterized by two features. 1. It is usually a relatively slow reaction, and 2. It produces by-products. That is, it would yield other compounds besides C and D. Though these by-products are in smaller quantities than C and D, the fact remains that they are there and may not be ignored.

Prosperity may then be classified by analogy as an organic reaction. The main products are: high standard of living, first-class services (mail, police protection, an efficient judicial system, ...), and a well-maintained infrastructure (roads, bridges, water, sewer, and a power grid), just to name a few.

As a naturalized citizen of the U. S., the author had enjoyed all the fruits of prosperity. Thank God for it.

As someone who had previously lived in another society, the author may even be able to appreciate it more than if born in it. Recall the saying: if you want to know about water, do not ask the fish.

American thinkers have raised some crucial points of interest.

Jon Meacham (NEWSWEEK, July 21, 2008, p. 30) in his article "More a Matter of Mystery than Magic," quotes the Protestant theologian Reinhold Niebuhr who wrote:

"Original sin is that thing about man which makes him capable of conceiving of his own perfection and incapable of achieving it . . . . Man's capacity for justice makes democracy possible; but man's capacity for injustice makes democracy necessary."

Evan Thomas in an article entitled: "Washington is Working Just Fine. It is us That's Broken," NEWSWEEK, March 8, 2010, p. 27, noted that:

> "The problem is not the system. It is us—our "get mine" culture of entitlement. It is hard to know exactly how or when we got this self-indulgent. The 60s are partly to blame. The triumph of individual and civil rights, a wondrous fulfillment of the true meaning of the Constitution, was too often perverted into an "I got my rights" sense of victimhood. The noble push of the New Deal and the Great Society to fight poverty and illness, ... hardened into the nonsensical defiance some tea partiers show when they shout, "keep your government hands off my Medicare." The . . . . explosion of free expression contributed to the sour and selfish "Me Decade" of the 1970s. The spurt of economic activity in the 1980s and 90s spawned a generation of . . . . profligate spenders in the shopping malls of America."

Dr. Andy Stanley (son of Dr. Charles Stanley) called the phenomenon "Assumption of Consumption," in the nationally-televised August 22, 2010 ceremony. Its title says it all.

Did these spending habits make people happy? Alice Park (TIME, July, 12, 2010, p. 24) cited data that rank the U. S. as the 26th among 89 countries in "positive feelings", a measure of population's happiness.

The above finding withstands the No.1 status in GDP per capita. Julia Baird in the article entitled: "Positively Downbeat," NEWSWEEK, October 5, 2009, p. 26, wrote:

> "while Europeans are growing happier, ... Americans are not. This is fascinating because it is in this country that a relentless focus on "positive thinking" . . . . has emerged over the past few decades—and it is this country that is now more gloomy."

Could it well be that happiness comes from the inside not the outside? It is an inner feeling of content, peace, and joy. Prosperity is a blessing to be enjoyed so long as it is kept in the right perspective. It is a means not the goal. Prosperity will psychologically fail us if we thought of it as being the ultimate goal.

How does this self-indulgence translate politically? Evan Thomas (NEWSWEEK, March 8, 2010, p. 27), explains:

> "Politicians have never been very good at asking for sacrifice from their constituents . . . . lately, politicians seem to have lost the most essential element of the art of governing—meaningful compromise. In its pure form, compromise means mutual sacrifice. On Capitol Hill, there is only getting: politicians vote for a bill if they get something, like a tax cut for an interest group or a pork-barrel project for their district. But they are not willing to give up anything. This is especially true where the other party is concerned. Partisanship has never been worse."

So, the best political system, with one party in power and the other watching, is being dragged to near paralysis—as many have commented.

George F. Will in his article: "The Basement Boys," NEWSWEEK, March 8, 2010, p.24, tackles a critical idiosyncrasy that seems to be a by-product of prosperity. He quotes Gary Cross, a Pennsylvania State University historian, who wonders:

> "Where have all the men gone?" The economy had disproportionately affected men. George Will wrote: This injury to men is particularly unfortunate because it may exacerbate, and be exacerbated by, a culture of immaturity among the young men who are reluctant to grow up . . . . A recent study found that 55 % of men between the age of 18 and 24 are living in their parents' homes as are 13 % of men between 25 and 34, compared to 8 % of women. George Will goes on to quote Gary Cross who argues that the culture of the boy-men today is less a life stage than a life style . . . . Permissive parenting made children less submissive, and the decline of deference coincided with the rise of consumer and media cultures celebrating the indefinite retention of the tastes and habits of childhood. The opening of careers to talented women has coincided with the attenuation of male role models in popular culture."

Powerful arguments. May I suggest adding another factor behind what George Will calls "The Basement Boys." The recession had undoubtedly affected men more than women. Men have a choice, though. They can succumb to the situation, live with their parents, and enjoy an endless youth. Or, they go out and find a job—even with a minimum-wage pay. The satisfaction of having a job—any job, surpasses its monetary return.

But those men figure out that their parents have enough resources to cover their grown-up children as well. They know they live in a wealthy and prosperous country and may even feel that the society owes them a decent living. So, why bother? Opportunities would come anyway.

Is the phenomenon a by-product of prosperity? Perhaps so.

In a more recent article in the Northwest Florida Daily News, January 6, 2011, p. A6, George Will talks about "Freedom carries new risks in an age of excess." He cites Daniel Akst's book, "We have Met the Enemy. Self Control in an Age of Excess." Akst notes that:

> "The problems of freedom and affluence . . . . are desirable problems. But they are problems . . . . American life resembles a "giant all-you-can-eat buffet" offering calories, credit, sex . . . . and other invitations to excess . . . . bad decisions about smoking, eating, drinking . . . . account for almost half of U. S. deaths in "our losing war with ourselves." George Will then went on to say: "Today capitalism has a bipolar disorder, demanding self-controlled workers yet uninhibited shoppers."

This line of thinking may shed some light on a persistent problem that has been reported over the last two or three decades: student grades and how do they compare with those of other countries.

Teachers, curriculum, number and length of school days have all received varying degrees of blame. One wonders if any of these is the real culprit.

Our three daughters attended public schools. They had a good education that enabled them to later graduate with degrees in Medicine, Engineering and Journalism. This is the same education system that is under attack. (It is true that we lived in a decent neighborhood with good schools.).

It may be possible for an "outsider" who had experienced another culture to see things from a different angle.

Learning has never been easy. It requires discipline, effort and seriousness. Motivation is the key word. Motivation to learn comes primarily from the parents who view learning as a basic requirement for a better future. It goes without saying that not all parents agree, and some have bought into the false sense of security or that the society owes them something. The children follow suit. Probably another by-product of prosperity and affluence.

Again, prosperity is the ultimate goal a society strives to achieve. A prosperous society is the envy of all others. Prosperity coupled with, or the result of, democracy is what humanity has long aspired to achieve. As with many other aspects of life, there are advantages and disadvantages. The advantages of prosperity far outweigh any shortcomings so long as the society diagnosis and treats the cause(s).

It has correctly been said that excellence and innovations are the jewels of the American culture. No effort should be spared to maintain and sustain these two pillars.

The 43rd President, Bill Clinton (TIME, December 6, 2010, p. 36) wrote:

> " . . . . people took for granted that nothing bad would happen, which is a luxury of living in a singularly fortunate land . . . . Florida Justice Leander Shaw wrote: "We are a nation of men and women and, although we aspire to lofty principles, our methods at times are imperfect." Clinton added: "That is human nature, and it will not change—and we would be wise to start preparing for it."

Regulation or No Regulation.

The Nobel laureate Niall Ferguson in an article entitled: "Wall Street's New Gilded Age," NEWSWEEK, September 21, 2009, p. 52, gave a historical account of the financial system in America. He wrote:

> "Since its birth the United States has grappled with the problem of an over mighty financial sector . . . . the Founders' vision was of a republic of self-reliant farmers and small-town trades men. The last thing they wanted was . . . . a mammon-worshiping metropolis in which financial capital and political capital were rolled into one."

> "That was why there was such resistance to creating a central bank, and why . . . . we have no Bank of the United States to match the Bank of England . . . . That was why there was so much suspicion when the Federal Reserve System was created in 1913. That was why government regulation of Wall Street was so strict from the Depression until the 1970s."

> "But now [September 2009] barely a year after one of the worst crises in all financial history, we seem to have returned to the Gilded Age of the late 19th century—the last time bankers came close to ruling America. A few Wall Street giants . . . . are back to making serious money and paying million-dollar bonuses."

The contrast is appalling as the unemployment rate hovered around 10 percent and home foreclosures keep rising almost three years after the bankruptcy of Lehman Brothers Holdings on 9/15/2008. In his 2009 article, Ferguson noted:

> "Last year's crisis . . . . established what had previously only been suspected—that the survivors were "too big to fail," effectively guaranteed by the full faith and credit of the United States. Yes, folks, now it is official: heads, they win; tails, we the taxpayers, lose. And in return, we get . . . . a $30 charge if we inadvertently run up a $ 1 overdraft with our credit card . . . . The "too big to fail" are able to pay crazy money because they reap all the rewards of risk-taking without the cost: the risk of going bust."

It has long been argued that the financial system can, and should, be left to control and manage itself without much interference from the government. The underlying assumption seemed appropriate for a free-market, capitalist society.

The question that emerges, though, is: can human nature be left unchecked? Can a society function without laws, police, and courts? Especially when it comes to money—more begets more. The overwhelming desire for possessions is an intrinsic human behavior.

The Creator has pointed out that one can not serve both God and mammon, and that the love of money is the root of much evil.

The last financial crisis of 2008 left no much doubt about the need for regulation. Does the Financial Reform Bill passed in the Summer of 2010 go far enough? The future would tell.

CHAPTER 25

A BLESSED JOURNEY

It has been 30 years since we arrived, on March 4, 1981, to the United States. A lifetime in itself.

Thank God who gave us the courage to take the decision of leaving the comfort of an extended family, friends, and a familiar culture to move to the U. S. It is true that very many people aspire to living in America—the most powerful, prosperous country in mankind's history. But at the time, the author, the head of the family, had to weigh a number of considerations.

My wife and I were in our early forties—not quite young in the eyes of American employers. Our graduate and post-graduate degrees were from overseas. We had three children aged 10 and eight years; the youngest was seven months.

If this was not enough, consider the fact that, at the time, the U. S. was going through one of the "two worst recessions (those of 1981 to 82 and 1973 to 75, with peak unemployment of 10.8 percent and 9 percent, respectively)," as Robert J. Samuelson reported in NEWSWEEK, March 31, 2008, p. 58.

We were aware that dollars do not grow on trees for people to pick up—even in America.

Why would an employer hire, or even consider, someone educated in another country at a time when the job market provided an abundance of domestically-educated ones?

All were legitimately-posed questions. A certain degree of risk was involved even for an optimistic person like the author. The odds were stacked against us. If it was only me, I would have had no hesitation going forward, but with a wife and three young daughters the burden was not light, and the risks had to be pondered.

One can not ignore a major force that goaded the author to make up his mind.

Egypt had lately gone through some tough times—socially, economically, and politically. The most detrimental was the socioeconomic environment. Many had seen the rapid deterioration of an otherwise friendly, generous, and hospitable society. And as the pie got smaller and smaller, some of the ties that characterized the social fabric became frayed. The future seemed to lack any glimmer of hope.

One thing that strikes the author, and I believe many others, is how Hollywood fails to accurately portray the American society. Those who have never been to America rely on movies and TV programs as the window through which they may have a peek at the country that has captivated the world's imagination with its ideals, democracy, prosperity, and innovations. In the eyes of many, America has been associated with anything and everything that is new—a symbol of newness.

But this is not what Hollywood portrays. Sex, blood, and violence are the common themes. And this is not America. Chasing the buck, not reality, seem to be the motivation for many in the movie industry.

A newcomer to the United States encounters a conservative, law-abiding citizenry. A society that does its best at assimilating those who had just moved in. A society that treats all its citizens equally under the law, according to the Constitution. A country whose citizens settle their differences in court.

In "A Call to Greatness" article (TIME, September 13, 2010, p. 42), Tony Blair wrote:

> "There is a nobility in the American character that has been developed over the centuries .... That nobility .... is a feeling about the country. It is a devotion to the American ideal that at a certain point transcends class, race, religion or upbringing. That ideal is about values: freedom, the rule of law, democracy. It is also about

> the way you achieve: on merit, by your own efforts and hard work. But it is most of all that in striving for and protecting that ideal, you as an individual take second place to the interests of the nation as a whole."

A Romanian named Cornel Nistorescu wrote an article with a title that means "Ode To America" that was published in the Romanian Newspaper "The Daily Event" or "News of the Day." Some excerpts from the Internet:

> "Why are Americans so united? They would not resemble one another even if you painted them all one color! They speak all the languages of the world and form an astonishing mixture of civilizations and religious beliefs."

> "On 9/11, the American tragedy turned 300,000,000 people into a hand put on the heart. Nobody rushed to accuse the White House, the Army . . . . Nobody rushed to empty their bank accounts . . . . After the first moments of panic, they raised their flag over the smoking ruins . . . . On every occasion, they started singing : God Bless America . . . . How on earth were they able to respond united as one human being? . . . . What on earth unites the Americans in such a way? Their land? Their history? Their economic power? Money? . . . . I reached but one conclusion . . . . Only freedom can work such miracles."

Who would have a better feeling for freedom than someone who had lived under one of the most repressive regimes in the world—even among those of the Soviet-bloc nations. What Nistorescu may have overlooked in his search for the unity and greatness of America is a culture built on Christianity.

Christianity is not just a religion but a way of life. Our Lord Jesus Christ did not give us merely a list of dos and do-nots, but had one request: that the human being gives his/her heart to God. Everything else falls in place. It is that simple. A decision to be made. God has created us free to choose: to be with Him or not. He does not force any one to worship Him. The Creator, in His love for the human race, decided to grant us the honor and dignity to decide for ourselves.

Over the three years of His ministry on earth, He did all the miracles that the mind can think of. His teachings embraced all the noble notions of love, forgiveness, meekness, kindness, and caring for the weak. He knew our weak nature would trammel us from always obeying His commandments, but those who love Him are aware of what they should have done when they fail.

A society that feeds upon Christian edification is likely to live in harmony to achieve greatness.

One of the great achievements of the United States is the education system—especially higher education. Lamar Alexander, now a U. S. Senator who was U. S. Education Secretary for George H. W. Bush, president of the University of Tennessee, and governor of Tennessee, wrote an article entitled: "The Three Year Solution," NEWSWEEK, October 26, 2009, p. 26, about how the "Three Year Solution" could benefit parents, students, and schools. In the article, he quotes the former Brazilian President Fernando Henrique Cardeso when asked what memory he would take back to Brazil about his year as scholar-in-residence in the United States. The former Brazilian President replied: "The American University, the greatness and the autonomy of the American University. There is nothing in the world quite like it."

The autonomy and a massive government funding that showered "money on research and development, and channeled most of it through universities [was] a brilliant innovation that has endured as an American model," wrote Fareed Zakaria in NEWSWEEK, November 23, 2009, p. 38. It is a source of national pride to know that for 2009: of the 13 people honored as Nobel-Prize winners nine were Americans. "The country still dominates the fields of information technology, life sciences, and nanotechnology, all key industries of the future," Zakaria reported.

The first-class services and superbly-maintained infrastructure of America exceeded all expectations. For those who criticize or claim otherwise, one would suggest a trip to another country.

At this stage of life (the 70s) the author often sits back and try to evaluate the successes and failures we, as a family, have gone through.

A few failures are less the norm than an aberration. Failures are a fact of life. But the net effect is gleefully positive. As a family, we are healthy, our daughters and sons-in-law are happy in their lives and careers. The grandchildren are a tremendous source of joy to their parents and, of course, to their grandparents.

Dawlat and I are retired, and live in the Florida panhandle (paradise) with its white sand and clear, blue water (yes, we were spared the aftermath of the Gulf oil spill).

To whom goes the credit? To the author taking responsibility, working hard, and planning? To my wife who nurtured our daughters especially in the inchoate years of our stay in the United States?

As parents we did what any parents would have done. But it is the Lord who blessed us. He opened the doors in front of the author to get the first job in the U. S. at a time when the country was in one of its worst recessions (1981 to 1982). He guided the author to get back into research—my favorite career. A United States patent and a Fulbright scholarship were a gift from Him as one considers the circumstances associated with each.

Dawlat had gone through a parallel path. Her first job in America was a baby-sitter (requires a Ph. D. degree in physics?). She studied computer programming while working as a pharmacy technician. Through a series of events she got a computer-programming position. Two promotions followed before retiring as a senior programmer analyst for the State of Kansas.

We firmly believe that God's hand was, and is, behind our long, but successful, journey.

It has been a blessed journey.

In his insightful book "My Utmost for His Highest," Oswald Chambers wrote, in effect: If He made your cup sweet, drink it with grace; if He made it sour, share it with others.

Though undeserving, He made the cup sweet.

May the Lord grant us the wisdom to walk humbly in His presence.

A final thought to ponder:

The renowned, contemporary Christian apologist Ravi Zacharias said:

"When you love someone and he does not love you back, you hurt because you lost something. When God loves you and you do not love Him back, God hurts, not because He lost anything, but because YOU lost something."